★ SERGEANT ★
STUBBY

HOW A STRAY DOG *and* HIS BEST FRIEND
HELPED WIN WORLD WAR I *and*
STOLE *the* HEART *of a* NATION

ANN BAUSUM

NATIONAL GEOGRAPHIC

Washington, D.C.

For the generations—
My parents, Dolores and Henry
My sons, Jake and Sam

Published by the National Geographic Society
1145 17th Street N.W., Washington, D.C. 20036

ISBN: 978-1-4262-1310-6

Founded in 1888, the National Geographic Society is one of the world's largest non-profit scientific and educational organizations. With a mission to inspire people to care about the planet, the member-supported Society offers a community for members to get closer to explorers, connect with other members and help make a difference. The Society reaches more than 500 million people worldwide each month through *National Geographic* and other magazines; National Geographic Channel; television documentaries; films; books; DVDs; radio; maps; exhibitions; live events; school publishing programs; interactive media; and merchandise. National Geographic has funded more than 10,000 scientific research, conservation and exploration projects and supports an education program promoting geographic literacy. For more information, visit www.nationalgeographic.com.

National Geographic Society
1145 17th Street N.W.
Washington, D.C. 20036-4688 U.S.A.

For information about special discounts for bulk purchases, please contact National Geographic Books Special Sales: ngspecsales@ngs.org

For rights or permissions inquiries, please contact National Geographic Books Subsidiary Rights: ngbookrights@ngs.org

Interior design: Katie Olsen

Printed in the United States of America

14/QGF-CML/1

★ CONTENTS ★

A SOLDIER'S BEST FRIEND

I AM A FIFTH-GENERATION U.S. MILITARY COMBAT VETERAN from Saint Simons Island, Georgia. Military service is in my blood—my father served as a United States Army ranger, his father before him served in the Navy during World War II as a patrol torpedo "PT" boat commander in the South Pacific, my great-grandfather served as an infantryman in the Army during World War I (alongside Stubby), and my great-great-great-great-grandfather served in the Revolutionary War. My service is part family lineage, part innate desire to serve my country.

Today, I am 34 years old and married to my magnificent and beautiful wife, Jenny (also a U.S. Military veteran), and a father to my amazing two-year-old son, Dax. I'm also the proud owner of my dog, Cheyenne. Cheyenne was a gift from God and one of the most important reasons I am still here today.

My military service began in 1999, when I served for six years in the United States Air Force Security Forces. During my service I endured several incidents that, at the time, I thought wouldn't affect my personal relationships with family, friends, and colleagues. A short time after arriving in Saudi Arabia in November 2001 for my first deployment in support of Operation Enduring Freedom, I encountered a Taliban sympathizer in a one-to-one confrontation. His weapon was pointed directly in my face during an Entry Control Point Check. At that very moment, I felt paralyzed—as if the world around me froze in time and all I could think about was surviving the next minute, getting out of that shack and back to my hometown. I had never had a weapon pointed at me, yet alone directly in my face, and all I could do was freeze. Then I remembered my father telling me to remain calm and breathe.

I remember signaling to the man that I was going to lay down my weapon. I took off the combat sling placed diagonally across my chest and threw my weapon at the guard, causing him to drop his gun to avoid being hit in the face by my weapon. It was then that I tackled him. His five-foot-four-inch frame was no match for me at six foot six. While graciously providing him with a few "love taps" of my elbow, I subdued him with a pair of plastic handcuffs while I waited for my leadership to arrive.

A second incident occurred three years later while I was on patrol in an undisclosed location within Pakistan. I noticed what appeared to be two suicide bombers directly outside the perimeter of the base, and they seemed determined to cross the razor wire barrier with a ladder. One of the men was pointing at the food tent area while wearing a belt of explosives strapped to his chest. Not willing to allow these two men to succeed with a suicide bombing attack against us, my team and I quickly foiled their plan of killing or injuring American troops.

This time I felt angry as I tried to reconcile why American troops were in a region where our presence was not wanted. Even the foreign military partners we worked alongside expressed their desire for us to be gone. "We want all of you to go home now," they would say. I can see now that a lot of my anger stemmed from this situation.

Upon returning from my first deployment to Saudi Arabia in March 2002, I began to act violently toward my family, friends, and even myself. I found myself waking up in the middle of the night with cold sweats, and I would randomly break down, crying uncontrollably, and blame and question myself on how or why I had handled the life-threatening situations I had found myself in overseas. Eight years later I would come to understand that these were all symptoms of post-traumatic stress disorder (PTSD) and depression, which I was eventually diagnosed with. However, my life would get much worse before it would improve.

It was around this time that I adopted a young pit bull mix from a rescue in Hampton Roads, Virginia. I named her Cheyenne and I hoped having her would add some purpose to my life. One afternoon in 2002, I finally hit rock bottom on the bedroom floor of my apartment. I sat, legs folded, ready to finish the fight with the demons that had followed me back from the war zone and had been a constant torment: the sudden rages, the punched walls, the profanities tossed at anyone who tried to help me. There was nothing in my room other than dirty military uniforms, some empty bottles of alcohol, and a crushing despair. I took a deep breath. I shut my eyes and tightly closed my lips around the cool steel of my .45 caliber pistol—the same pistol my father bestowed upon me after my completion of military technical training, the pistol my father was issued for his 1966 training in the U.S. Army's Ranger School. And then something licked my ear. I looked around and locked eyes with Cheyenne. With her head cocked to one side she looked at me as only a dog can, with her big brown eyes full of devotion, as if to say, "What are you doing? Who's going to take care of me? Who else is going to let me sleep in your bed?"

For a long minute, I stared into the puzzled face of my six-month-old pit bull. And then slowly, reluctantly, I backed the barrel of my .45 caliber pistol out of my mouth. There is no doubt about it, I owe Cheyenne my life.

Immediately I felt so relieved, like a 10,000-pound weight had been lifted off my chest. Soon after, my family and friends noticed a significant change in my behavior—a reduced number of outbursts, a better attitude, and no more attempts at my life—all because of this little pit bull puppy. Cheyenne's heroics were her unconditional love and devotion to me, a devotion and love that most pet owners can attest to. Devotion that Stubby had his entire life for his best friend and for the soldiers he went to war with. It's interesting that a torn-eared puppy from a shabby animal rescue saved me. Not my father, or my grandfather, or my friend who endured the same scars of combat while serving alongside me. Cheyenne was the force who pulled me back into society. I couldn't talk to anybody—not my father, not the counselors—but I could talk to my dog, and she never judged me. Eight years later, my father said to me, "You're a different person now. All that stuff was taking over your life, son. That dog just listened to you for hours." Until Cheyenne, I had suffered in silence.

In January 2010, with the help of a friend, I walked into the Washington, D.C., Veterans Affairs Hospital for the first time to seek additional help in my life. The process to diagnose my PTSD and depression was a very frustrating and time-intensive gauntlet; however, it was worth it. There was some fear about speaking to a person about my military service for the first time, and I was somewhat apprehensive. But Cheyenne helped me become an extrovert, and so telling another person, or persons, proved to not be as difficult as I thought it would be.

When man and dog can stare death in the face, like Cheyenne and I did, like Stubby and the soldiers of World War I did, and forge on with their lives and their duty to their country, that is the true testament to the bond we share with these animals.

One year later, I married Jenny Fritcher, an Air Force staff sergeant stationed at Ramstein Air Base in Germany. My wife is now months away from graduating with a bachelor's degree in nursing, and she will soon reenter the U.S. military as a nurse, to help take care of our troops. She has inspired me to pursue my dream of becoming a physician's assistant so that I may also aid my fellow soldiers in tackling the mental anguish that stems from their military service.

As much as my formal counseling helped me, I know that all the credit for my mental well-being goes to Cheyenne. With her unconditional love I became a resilient and productive member of society.

The story you will discover on the following pages about a stray dog named Stubby shows the true humanity of war and the bond that can be borne between a dog and a soldier, even in the most horrific of conditions. Ann Bausum has uncovered the seemingly forgotten story of Stubby and brought to life the engrossing details of devotion and courage that Stubby showed throughout his life to his fellow soldiers.

With the support Cheyenne provided me as inspiration, I set out on a mission in 2009, with only $2,500 in my savings account, to create the nonprofit organization Companions For Heroes. Companions For Heroes pairs active-duty military, veterans, and emergency first responders dealing with the stress of their service with shelter animals as part of their healing process. My hope was that others would find solace, comfort, and strength in a shelter animal of their choosing, like I found in Cheyenne. In fact, a July 2011 study published in the *Journal of Personality and Social Psychology* revealed that pet owners had greater self-esteem, had greater levels of exercise and physical fitness, and tended to be less lonely than non-owners. These are exactly the qualities needed by veterans with mental health disorders, and my goal for Companions For Heroes is to aid veterans in their recovery while at the same time saving our nation's shelter animals. As Stubby provided strength and comfort to the soldiers of World War I, I believe Cheyenne and all the animals that have been adopted through Companions For Heroes, in some small fraction, are carrying on Stubby's legacy.

—David E. Sharpe
Disabled Combat Veteran, U.S. Air Force Security Forces
Founder and Chairman, Companions For Heroes
www.companionsforheroes.org

INTRODUCTION

THIS MUCH I KNEW FOR SURE: THERE WAS A WAR. THERE was a soldier. And there was a dog.

I discovered the dog by accident in late 2009. He wandered into my world in much the same way he had wandered into the history of World War I—randomly, unplanned, unanticipated, and with wonderful consequences. I was researching a photo caption for a book about that war, and I needed some instant information about one of the dogs pictured in a political cartoon, a so-called American bull terrier. To my surprise, an Internet search started turning up random sites about a dog named Sergeant Stubby. The animal's story seemed so incredible that at first I did not believe it could be true.

The sites claimed that the dog had contributed heroically to the outcome of World War I, a war so horrendously destructive that it had claimed the lives of more than 100,000 Americans in a matter of months, and yet somehow Stubby had survived. How could one dog have been so capable, endured such dreadful combat, and gained such fame? And yet those were Stubby's claims: Veteran of 17 battles, captured a German spy, shook hands with President Woodrow Wilson, et cetera, et cetera. Seriously? Surely someone had made him up. And then I clicked on a link from the Smithsonian. And there he was. Catalog Number 58280M, lifelike and ready for action. Lifelike and ready to befriend someone new.

In the years since our initial acquaintance, Sergeant Stubby, the character I first encountered, has become just plain old Stubby to me, shorn of the military rank that has been bestowed on him in recent years by his fans and the power of the Internet in the age of (mis)information. In his lifetime, and for generations afterward, the dog didn't need a rank to be adored, and he doesn't for me, either.

Full disclosure: I am not a dog person. All of the dogs from my childhood met tragic ends. Pooh the cocker spaniel: hit by a car. Benet the Chihuahua: disappeared. Checkers the Dalmatian: hit by the mail truck. Checkers II, another Dalmatian: put to sleep as the result of illness. By the time I'd reached adulthood, I'd grown to dislike dogs. They slobbered a lot, made family members sneeze, and chased my outdoor cats. With the exception of Pooh, I'd never truly bonded with a dog, so the idea of writing a book about one was beyond improbable.

Then I met Stubby.

One thing I've learned after 15 years of writing nonfiction is that I don't choose my topics so much as they choose me. It's the ideas that I can't get out of my head that end up on my computer screen. Stubby grabbed hold of me in the way good stories do: with a smile, coming to mind unexpectedly, and showing up with growing frequency. Doggedly, one could say. Stubby wandered into my head with the endearing persistence of a pet anticipating the arrival of the dinner hour. "Are you ready yet?" he seemed to ask each time. "Is it my turn?" Until finally it *was* his turn and I *was* ready to dive into his story.

I knew it would be a challenge. The trail of Stubby's past had long since grown cold. He was famous for his role in World

*As his fame grew, Stubby learned how to pose for photographers.
In 1924 he paused for pictures on the White House lawn
following a visit with President Calvin Coolidge.*

War I, for goodness' sake, and the entire trail of World War I seemed to have gone cold. How could I expect to learn about one dog out of thousands who had befriended one soldier out of millions in a fight that had occurred an ocean away, a fight that had largely been erased from the national conscience of the fighters' home country?

However, having become captivated by Stubby's story, I stepped willingly into my sleuthing shoes and headed into the fifth dimension of the past. My travels took me to Washington, D.C., for work at the Smithsonian and Georgetown University. They drew me to the National World War I Museum in Kansas City, Missouri; the cities and countryside of Connecticut; the campus of Yale University; and the archives of the U.S. Army War College in Carlisle, Pennsylvania. I dipped my face into the Internet "pensieve" of archived news clippings, and cherished war medals, and maps of battlefield landmarks. The deeper I dug, the more leads I found, until by chance and good fortune I discovered living descendants of Stubby's best friend and caregiver—J. Robert Conroy—and answers to questions that had otherwise eluded capture in the historical record.

As I began to research the life of Stubby, I rather thought my arm's length personal view of dogs might add objectivity to my work, but I would be dishonest to maintain this claim. Instead my subject charmed me just as he had charmed the soldiers of World War I, the news writers of the day, and every U.S. President of his lifetime. Halfway through my research I found myself checking books out of the library that were totally unrelated to my project. How to choose a dog, profiles for different breeds of dogs, how to care for a dog, and so on. For no rational reason, I, the dog hater, began to think about acquiring a dog.

That is the power of Stubby.

One of the many visits I made while under Stubby's spell was to the storage areas of the Smithsonian's National Museum of American History. I wanted to see a jacket that Stubby had worn, and a curator kindly indulged me. This garment is stored in a flat box with a protective sunken center. I'd seen it on Stubby's back in countless photos. Now it looked oddly unrelated, all flattened and sterile. And yet, even after all these years, the jacket gives off faint smells—some sort of custom blending of leather, and dog, and Army, and history.

Follow your noses, readers, and turn the pages of this book. Meet this dog. He was just a stray dog, a brave stray adopted by an American soldier. A dog who went on to become the most famous dog of the Great War, the War to End All Wars, World War I. A brave dog. A loyal dog. A lovable dog.

Here is his story.

PART ONE

TWO RECRUITS

During World War I, J. Robert Conroy served in the Headquarters Company for the 102nd Infantry Regiment of the Yankee Division, shown here, stateside, in 1917. His canine friend Stubby became the regiment's mascot and served alongside the troops in France.

April 20, 1918

★ ★ ★ ★ ★

First comes the rain. One of those cold, penetrating showers that falls in early spring, unhurried and endless. Hour after hour the men of the 102nd hunker down in the rising mud of the Sibille trench, trying to sleep through another night of war. Sentries strain to hear hints of warning, having lost the use of their eyes to a shroud of fog.

Then the shelling commences. At 3 a.m. the Germans begin to lob relentless rounds at the American troops near Seicheprey. The figure of Death extends a fistful of options. Obliterated by an artillery shell. Drained of life force after being cut to pieces by shrapnel. Subdued by clouds of poisonous gas.

Or await the waves of German troops that approach at dawn in a foggy curtain of mist and smoke.

The bombardment has already thinned the ranks of C and D companies by the time the enemy arrives. Waves of German shock troops wash over the trench battlement, eager to rout the American reinforcements who have come to help defend the rain-soaked soil of France. Dreadfully outnumbered, the Yankee boys of the 102nd still fight back.

Hand-to-hand combat lasts for one hour, two hours, longer, until none remain standing to hold the line.

April 20, 1918

One trench down.

The Germans advance toward Seicheprey and the next line of defenses, still outnumbering those detailed for protection.

More men. More men. The Allies need more men.

So, as German gunners adjust their lines of shelling, every able-bodied soul heads forward from the rear. All hands called to arms.

Infantrymen. Officers. Messengers. More.

Forms head toward the action, clutching bayonet-tipped rifles.

Fresh troops.

Fresh troops. Groups of men. Individual men. One man.

And a dog.

CHAPTER ONE

A DOG'S BEST FRIEND

IN THE BEGINNING, SOMEONE CARED ENOUGH ABOUT THE dog to cut off his tail.

The brindle-patterned pup probably owed at least some of his parentage to the evolving family of Boston terriers, a breed so new that even its name was in flux. Boston round heads. American bull terriers. Boston bull terriers. Regardless of name, a truncated tail became a trademark of the breed, and one way that early enthusiasts achieved that look was to dock, or cut off, the bulk of it soon after birth. Thus, the fact that the dog had passed through human hands at some point early in his life was evident by his lack of a tail. What came next was as much a mystery in 1917 as it is today. By the time the stump-tailed terrier of uncertain breeding had found his way to the athletic fields of Yale University, he was nameless, tailless, and homeless.

His arrival at Yale coincided with America's entry into World War I, a confluence of circumstances that propelled the dog onto the path of history. On April 6, 1917, the U.S. Congress declared war on Germany, entering a three-year-old conflict that would become known as the Great War and the War to End All Wars, before earning the designation of World War I. The next month, President Woodrow Wilson signed legislation that required all able-bodied men aged 21 to 30 to register for possible military service. In the months that followed, Connecticut's volunteers and draftees wound up in New Haven, where Yale University had opened its athletic fields for use as a training ground.

Everything seemed to be in transition—the nation, the war, the expanding American Army, even the campuses of its colleges and universities—and it became easy to throw a stray dog into the mix. Some say the dog with a stub of a tail already lived around Yale's athletic stadium before the troops began arriving in July 1917. If he didn't, it wouldn't have taken him long to figure out that he should. It took a lot of food to feed a camp full of active men, and that meant a lot of cooking went on, day after day. And *that* meant a stray dog could enjoy an endless supply of bones, and scraps, and scrounging.

Although the dog the soldiers nicknamed "Stubby" was not the only stray who lived off the leavings of the men's meals, he does seem to have been among the most likable, and probably he was exceptionally clever. He was a handsome enough dog— muscular, wiry, solid—standing not quite two feet tall on all fours, measuring a bit more than two feet long from snout to stubby tail. His coat was a sandy brown color, streaked with waves of darker fur. White patches highlighted his chest and face, emphasizing his dark nose and eyes. White fur capped his front feet, too, and it lightly frosted his back paws.

The dog was just old enough for his age to be unclear. Bigger than a puppy, too active for an old dog, he might have been a year or two years of age in 1917. Before long the mysterious stray had become a spunky pal for the service members, an animal who could be counted on to visit camp tents, add his steps to military training exercises, and memorize the locations of the mess kitchens.

Soon Stubby had picked out his favorite soldier in the crowd: James Robert Conroy. The 25-year-old volunteer from New Britain, Connecticut, was a man of modest height with brown eyes, a thick head of dark hair, and a winning smile. A few sparse facts constitute his recorded background. His mother, Alice C. McAvay, had been born in Pennsylvania to Irish immigrants before her family moved to New Britain. His father, James P. Conroy, a native of that city, had tried his hand at the family grocery business and as the owner of a saloon before becoming a local bookkeeper in the 1890s.

The pair married about 1887, and they settled into a modest home on Beaver Street. During the span of 11 years, they had six children. James Joseph, the third child and the first son, was born on February 27, 1892. (By the time he enlisted in the military the young man had, for unrecorded reasons, renamed himself James Robert, shortened to J. Robert and, among friends, Bob.) Another son, Hugh, followed four years later, and the youngest siblings, twin girls, were born in 1898 when the eldest boy was six. A year later, their father died. Nearby relatives, including several of Alice's brothers and her widowed mother, appear to have helped her raise her family. After her own mother died, Alice moved her offspring into their grandmother's larger house on High Street, and the family remained there while the children grew up.

James Robert Conroy attended local public schools and graduated from high school in 1910. Three years later, when he was 21, his mother died. Conroy stayed on in the family home, helping his elder sisters support and raise the three youngest children. After high school, he found work with Russell & Erwin Manufacturing Company, a local firm known for its well-crafted builders' hardware, especially door locks and hinges. Conroy quickly

The first known photo of Stubby with Robert Conroy:
Already the dog is part of the family. Conroy (standing, center)
is joined by two of his sisters in this group shot taken during
the summer of 1917 at the regimental training ground
on the athletic fields of Yale University.

graduated from the factory floor to a series of appointments that sent him to Pittsburgh (as a sales representative), to New York City (where he worked in the company's contracts department), and to Springfield, Massachusetts (for more sales work).

The war drew Conroy away from his established career post. On Monday, May 21, 1917, he enlisted in the Connecticut National Guard, just three days after President Wilson's call for the start of registration. Plenty of young men waited for the June registration deadline and the lottery that would determine whether or not they would be called up for duty, but not Conroy. He had already served in the state's guard once before, for about a year starting in April 1913, soon after the death of his mother. This time Conroy volunteered to serve the organization as a mounted scout. His National Guard outfit was soon renamed the 102nd Infantry Regiment, and its men trained together in New Haven prior to shipping out for Europe.

Stubby continued to roam the grassy grid of Camp Yale "streets," visiting other friends and feeding posts, but he took a special liking to Conroy, and Conroy clearly took a shine to him. In the following months, the pair bonded until they became almost inseparable. Looking after an agreeable dog suited Conroy's nature. Hanging around a kind human suited Stubby's. The fact that there was a war to prepare for certainly meant nothing to the dog, and even Conroy and his fellow trainees could barely imagine what they were preparing to encounter.

The nature of warfare had changed by the time of the Great War, resulting in odd juxtapositions of old and new ways of fighting. Clouds of poisonous chlorine gas commingled with the familiar smoke and smell of gunpowder. Silent submarines sneaked up on coal-fired steamships. Machine-gunners fired on meagerly protected adversaries, clad only in fabric uniforms. Soldiers maneuvered tanks onto battlefields shared by cavalry officers on horseback. Pilots flew airplanes over war zones that were criss-crossed by messenger pigeons. Train engines hauled enormous railway guns into positions while horses, mules, and other draft animals strained to deliver artillery pieces to gun batteries.

This mismatch of equipment and strategy led to the invention of a new way of fighting. Soldiers dug trenches and bunkers so they could hide belowground away from the artillery and machine-gun fire. They created miles and miles of trenches, in fact. Trenches that spanned lengthy stretches of the disputed European borders. Trenches that became, by default, borders of their own. The "No Man's Land" between the opposing sides offered the likelihood of death to many who entered it.

Battlefront survivors struggled to cope with the facial disfiguring, physical disabilities, and emotional trauma that resulted from that era's modern-style warfare. It would take another half century to coin the phrase post-traumatic stress disorder (PTSD), but the veterans of World War I suffered from that condition, too. They called it, simply, shell shock, and they did not begin to understand how insidious it was, or how long-lasting it could be.

Before the Americans arrived, France, Britain, and other Allied countries had already dedicated hundreds of thousands of their ablest young men in futile contests along the trench-lined battle zone. By 1917, their best hope for turning the tide of war became the promise of fresh troops from the United States.

For reasons about as obscure as Stubby's origins, Conroy and the other U.S. infantrymen of World War I became known as doughboys. Maybe it's because the American foot soldiers ate a lot of doughnuts, or perhaps they made more "dough" than their European allies. Some suggest the name arose during a 1916 U.S. military campaign into Mexico. It is said that American cavalry troops stirred up so much dust while they pursued the invading Mexican revolutionary Pancho Villa that the accompanying foot

*Fighter planes debuted for military service during
World War I, but soldiers continued to employ an older
technology, too—aerial observation balloons. These craft
were generally tethered while they hovered over battlefields.
Observers radioed such details as the location of trench lines
and gun batteries to ground forces.*

soldiers became coated in the local adobe-colored soil; the cavalry nicknamed their dirty compatriots adobe-boys, or simply "dough-boys." One way or the other, by 1917 the name had stuck to American infantrymen as persistently as a coat of swirling dust.

During the summer of 1917, Stubby charmed Conroy and the other doughboys stationed in New Haven, Connecticut. He was by all accounts a wonderful dog, cheerful, faithful, friendly, lovable. He formed an intense loyalty to men in uniform, at least men wearing a U.S. military uniform.

While the soldiers trained, Stubby studied the scene. He learned the meanings of the various bugle calls that set the pace of the day, from reveille to taps, with mess call becoming a personal favorite. The dog became used to the rhythms of the regimental marching band during its daily practices, and he learned how to follow along with soldiers as they paraded in formation on the athletic fields of Yale University. In short, Stubby learned how to be a perfectly good soldier, albeit, one with four legs.

Most notable of all his training, perhaps, was Stubby's signature trick: He could salute. Conroy probably gets credit for teaching the dog this mandatory military gesture of greeting and respect. Stubby could perform the maneuver on command or in response to another soldier's delivery of the trademark hand wave. To salute, Stubby would sit down, rear up on his back legs, raise his right paw to the right side of his face, and gaze seriously at his counterpart until his gesture of respect had been answered. Hearts melted, and members of Conroy's unit soon regarded the talented dog as their mascot.

In some ways, Stubby's training was more complete than that of his doughboy companions. The U.S. Army struggled as it sought to swell its ranks from thousands of men to more than four million. In particular the soldiers lacked training in the use of military weapons, because, in many cases, no weapons were available for them to train with. As factories (including Conroy's former employer) retooled and rushed to catch up with demand, foot soldiers made do, using out-of-date rifles left over from the Spanish-American War of 1898, or even wooden props. Meanwhile, artillery and machine-gunners imagined themselves loading and firing their weapons by practicing with sawhorses and sticks.

The men balanced the lack of military fire power by practicing the rudiments of warfare. They dug trenches, built barriers out of barbed wire, and lunged with bayonets at dummies. Plus, as with any war, there was endless physical conditioning. The doughboys counted out jumping jacks, pushups, and other calisthenics. Day in and day out, they marched in parade drills or strapped on heavy backpacks and trudged to nowhere and back.

Week after week, Stubby hiked alongside the troops by day, visited the soldiers in their tents at night, and rose to the next dawn's call of reveille, punctuating the routine with regular trips to the camp kitchens. And so things might have continued forever, as far as Stubby was concerned, except for one huge problem, totally unknowable within the live-in-the-moment world of a dog: There was a war to fight.

★ CHAPTER TWO ★

OVER THERE

ON JUNE 28, 1914, A YOUNG SERBIAN RADICAL UNCORKED simmering nationalistic tensions in Europe by assassinating Archduke Franz Ferdinand, the heir to the Austro-Hungarian Empire. This act set off a chain reaction of brinksmanship and bluster that escalated into combat, thus triggering the tangled web of international alliances that drew other countries into the conflict that became the Great War.

Fighting began in early August as Austria-Hungary attacked Serbia and as Germany overran most of Belgium and parts of France. In short order, the Central Powers of Germany and Austria-Hungary, joined later on by the Ottoman Empire and Bulgaria, had squared off against the Allied Powers of France, Great Britain, Russia, and, later, Italy, among others.

Americans spent the next three years avoiding the war that was raging in Europe. In 1914, as soon as the fighting had erupted, President Woodrow Wilson had proclaimed United States–neutrality in the conflict. The war had its roots in Europe, he reasoned, along with many Americans, and so it was up to the European nations to resolve it. By 1916, Wilson had even earned a second term of office under the campaign slogan, "He kept us out of war!"

The President had another reason to avoid the war, too: the nation's diversity. In 1910, a third of the United States' residents were immigrants or the children of immigrants. Most of these people, and many of the country's established citizens, could trace their origins to the nations of Europe. The country that could claim the most offspring in America was none other than Germany itself. "We definitely have to be neutral," Wilson had concluded after the war broke out. "Otherwise our mixed populations would wage war on each other." He returned to this theme in his Second Inaugural Address. "We are of the blood of all the nations that are at war," he said on March 4, 1917, with the idea still serving as a compelling reason to remain detached from the conflict.

Germany tested Wilson's resolve repeatedly during his first administration, most notably with the sinking of a series of American and Allied ships. Submarines debuted as a lethal addition to sea power during the First World War, and Germany had one of the world's largest fleets of underwater craft. The rules of engagement for submarine power had yet to be created, so Germans tested the limits by attacking war ships (clearly fair game), supply ships (a plausible target), and the passenger ships of Allied nations (a controversial notion).

In 1915, Robert Conroy's employer transferred him from Pittsburgh to New York City. On May 7 of that same year, the sinking of a British ocean liner named the *Lusitania* drew widespread condemnation, in part because of the shocking destruction achieved by a single German torpedo. Unlike its sister ship the *Titanic,* which had languished above the waves for more than two hours after colliding with an iceberg in 1912, the *Lusitania* sank in only 18 terror-filled minutes. Nearly two-thirds of its occupants perished, including all of the infants on board and most of the children. The dead included 128 Americans.

Horror seized the public's imagination in a manner akin to the reaction that followed the terrorist attacks on September 11, 2001. The sinking of the *Lusitania*, too, was seen as an act of terror, and many voices called for revenge, including that of former President Theodore Roosevelt. Others, such as Secretary of State William Jennings Bryan, himself a three-time presidential candidate, counseled restraint. Wilson split the difference and called on the Germans to stop all aggression against non-military vessels. The "or else" implied in that directive prompted Bryan, a pacifist, to resign from office. He feared that Germany would never cede its naval rights to an outside power and that the United States would have to back up Wilson's words with force.

At first, though, Wilson's ultimatum worked. The almost universal condemnation of the *Lusitania*'s sinking, including harsh criticism of Kaiser Wilhelm II himself, prompted the German ruler to order greater restraint in the use of submarine power. No commercial vessels were to be targeted, he insisted. This ban lasted, with rare exception, for nearly two years.

By early 1917, though, as Conroy settled into his duties in Massachusetts, the fighting in Europe had reached a stalemate. The battle lines were literally entrenched, and the Allies owed their survival in part to the armaments and supplies that they purchased from the United States (creating an awkward commercial bounty for a nation that still claimed neutrality in the European conflict).

German naval officers fumed as they watched this material steam past on non-military ships bound for Allied ports. In an effort to gain the advantage, military leaders convinced the Kaiser to let them begin attacking all Allied vessels, military and otherwise. Yes, the United States would likely enter the war, but it would take the nation many months to mobilize its fighting forces, they reasoned. Meanwhile the Germans could cut the Allies' supply lifeline immediately and seize a strategic advantage. Additionally, Russia was growing weaker on the eastern front and German officers anticipated its impending defeat, an outcome that would allow soldiers from that battlefront to be redeployed in Western Europe to confront the fresh American troops. The result would be a race between a final flexing of the formidable German war machine and the mobilization of an untested American one.

The Kaiser announced on February 1, 1917, that his nation would soon resume open warfare on supply ships and other commercial steamers. Two days later, Wilson severed all ties with Germany. Did Conroy catch this news? If so, he would have known that the space between peace and war was narrowing. Even if he'd failed to notice this development, few in the country, from Conroy to the unknown person who had docked Stubby's tail, was likely to have missed the next one: the Zimmerman telegram.

This document surfaced in late February, shortly before Germany renewed its attacks on commercial vessels. Arthur Zimmerman, the German foreign minister, had sent a coded message to his country's ambassador in Mexico suggesting that he recruit that nation as Germany's ally in a war against the United States. He promised Mexico a financial reward and the restoration (after a presumed victory) of Mexico's former territory in Arizona, New Mexico, and Texas. Details of the covert plan surfaced after Great Britain intercepted Zimmerman's telegram. Thus, U.S. involvement in the conflict became inevitable, even for the President who had "kept us out of war."

On April 2, 1917, Wilson addressed members of Congress and proclaimed that "the world must be made safe for democracy." The United States had to join the European fight, he said, to achieve "the ultimate peace of the world and for the liberation of its people." Four days later, federal legislators declared war against

Germany in a vote of 455 to 56. Those who supported the move had worn American flag pins on their jacket lapels on the night of Wilson's call to arms. Opponents to the measure, such as Senator Robert "Fighting Bob" La Follette of Wisconsin, who wore no such symbol, were ridiculed as unpatriotic and disloyal. Home front tensions flared between patriots and pacifists, immigrants and native-born Americans, and beyond. They even infiltrated causes as diverse as the labor movement and the long-standing fight for woman suffrage.

As recruiters set about mustering an expanded U.S. Army, the secretary of war tapped Brig. Gen. John Joseph Pershing to lead the anticipated troops. General Pershing had become a household name the previous year during his pursuit of Mexican

Dogs and soldiers had a way of meeting up during the First World War, whether officially or more casually. In this image a dog seems to accompany U.S. First Division troops on the go during operations in the St. Mihiel salient, September 1918.

revolutionary Pancho Villa, but his military career included 19th-century service, too, ranging from participation in some of the government's final battles with Native Americans, to leadership of a unit of African-American "buffalo soldiers," to combat service alongside Theodore Roosevelt during the Spanish-American War. He had performed with distinction in the Philippines early in the 20th century, too.

In late May 1917, Pershing met with Wilson as his commander in chief and assembled a staff of military advisers; soon after, he and his team set sail for Europe. Their job was to coordinate with Allied commanders on how best to integrate an as-yet-assembled American fighting force into the war effort. Among those who served under his command were officers who would become household names in their own right during the next world war: George C. Marshall, Douglas MacArthur, George Patton. Even the ranks of volunteers and enlisted men would yield future leaders, among them Harry S. Truman, the 34-year-old captain of an artillery battery.

While Pershing and his staff established working relationships and plotted strategy with their European counterparts, commanders back in the States began to assemble what would eventually become known as the American Expeditionary Forces, or A.E.F. Just over 300,000 soldiers served in the regular Army and the National Guard before Wilson's call to arms. The nation would need to raise an Army of millions—an enormous logistical challenge—if it were to contribute a game-changing force to the war effort. (Eventually the United States mobilized more than four million men and sent some two million of its sons to Europe as the A.E.F.)

Pershing chose to organize his troops into military divisions of 28,000 members apiece. He designed the divisions to include multiple self-contained fighting units of infantry, artillery, and machine-gun strength. Initially these divisions and their internal battalions would fight alongside the Allied forces. Pershing's eventual goal was for them to fight independently as one coordinated American force.

Divisions were to be constituted, trained, equipped, and transported to Europe in waves, with further training planned after reaching the continent. Regions of the country with a strong National Guard presence, such as New England, had a jump on training and recruitment. As Robert Conroy and Stubby drilled with National Guardsmen on the athletic fields of Yale University, military staffers began to knit Conroy's unit into a larger fighting force made up of volunteers and conscripted men. They called it the 26th Division, and because it drew its corps from the New England states it became known as the Yankee Division, or YD for short.

Clarence Ransom Edwards, a 58-year-old major general who hailed from Ohio, became the commander of Conroy's division in the summer of 1917. Although an outsider, he earned the respect of the New Englanders through his parentage (his father had come from Massachusetts), his colloquial style of command, and his personal attention to his men. He knew many of the soldiers by name and treated them like family. The men returned the compliment by calling him "Daddy," and they became fiercely loyal.

Four infantry regiments made up the core of the Yankee Division, supplemented by an artillery brigade, a regiment of engineers, signal corps members, machine-gunners, and so on. For practical reasons, the various units mobilized and trained separately near their points of origin across New England. Conroy's 102nd Infantry Regiment, based in New Haven, grew along with the other regiments to the prescribed size of 3,700 men. The doughboys were organized into companies of 250 soldiers each. Four companies made up a battalion, and three battalions constituted a regiment. Each regiment had its own support and specialty troops, too, from artillery batteries to supply companies to medical support. It even had its own military band.

A separate company of headquarters staff members was assembled to help the regimental commander with administration and specialty tasks. These men would gather military intelligence, carry messages, and process prisoners of war, among other responsibilities. Conroy, who had volunteered to serve as a mounted scout, was assigned to the support staff for the headquarters company of the 102nd Regiment. Off-duty he may have been teaching Stubby how to salute, but on duty he was learning the ropes of military command.

The nation's fighting forces reflected its diversity as a land awash with immigrants. Conroy was one of some 3,000 residents from New Britain, Connecticut, who joined the war effort, voluntarily or otherwise. The rolls of soldiers from his hometown stretch from John Abate, born in Italy, to Joseph Zysek, a native of Russia. Others hailed from Poland, Persia (now known as Iran), Greece, Armenia, and countries that were then classified as enemy nations.

Overall almost a fifth of the members of the U.S. armed forces had been born overseas, and the overwhelming majority of those immigrant soldiers—70 percent—had spent fewer than ten years on American shores. Immigrants from Germany and Austria-Hungary who had not adopted United States citizenship were rejected from service. The rolls from Conroy's New Britain and elsewhere included African Americans, too; these troops were consigned to segregated units. Women served in the military, as well, but they worked in support roles, especially as nurses, in an era before females participated in combat.

The nature of combat during the Great War required a unique combination of manpower, animal power, and machinery. Yes, the fighting forces employed submarines, tanks, and airplanes.

But they couldn't have managed without horses, mules, and oxen, either. Harnessed animals were a part of everyday life at home, and so their presence in a war zone was taken for granted. They bore riders, pulled supply wagons, and conveyed mobile camp kitchens toward the front. They hauled ammunition, lugged rations to waiting soldiers, and transported troops by the wagon-load. Beasts of burden were everywhere during the inauguration of the modern age of weaponry.

And then there were the dogs. Although the United States was slow to embrace the role that these animals could play in a war zone, European nations were not. By the turn of the 20th century, innovative trainers in Germany, Great Britain, France, and other countries had begun preparing dogs for military and police work. When the war broke out, dogs were everywhere.

Le chien sentinelle à son poste

"*Le chien sentinelle a son poste*"—*the guard dog, on duty—*
reads the handwritten caption added to this snapshot
from the front lines of France during World War I.

Messenger dogs. Rescue dogs. Guard dogs. Dogs that delivered armaments. Dogs that delivered cigarettes to men in the trenches. Dogs that killed trench rats. Tens of thousands of dogs served during the war.

Although some breeds were especially popular—Airedales among the British and, for Germans, their namesake shepherd—soldiers went to war with collies and huskies, bulldogs and sheepdogs, retrievers and dogs that, as in Stubby's case, were of uncertain parentage. The U.S. military brought no corps of service dogs to the front, so it turned to its allies for canine aid.

Communication proved problematic during the Great War. Technologies such as radio transmission would be perfected in time for the Second World War. In theory, telephones proved useful during World War I, but enemy shelling often severed the hand-strung lines, making human runners, pigeons, and messenger dogs essential means of transmitting military orders and conveying reports from the field. Some dogs served as liaison messengers, trained to make round-trips between locations. Others acted as one-way couriers, carrying military orders or even containers of messenger pigeons to front-line outposts. Such duties put them at risk of injury, capture, and death as a matter of battlefield routine.

Rescue dogs cruised fresh battlefields in search of the wounded. They carried packs of self-serve supplies for use by conscious soldiers, including such items as bandages, water, painkillers, and whiskey. Medics relied on rescue dogs to help them bypass the corpses on a battlefield so that they could reach wounded men more efficiently: Dogs could sense with greater speed and accuracy than a human whether or not a lifeless form still remained alive. Rescue dogs were known, too, as Red Cross dogs (sometimes wearing the trademark symbol of medical assistance), sanitary dogs, and mercy dogs. In the latter role the animals offered comfort to the grievously wounded, serving as the final companions for dying soldiers.

Today people take it for granted that dogs and other animals contribute to the mental health of the troops both on and off the battlefield. No one had proven that connection at the time of World War I, but the anecdotal evidence was everywhere. Soldiers didn't just put animals to work; they turned them into mascots, companions, and friends. Meanwhile, soldiers overseas adopted not just dogs but cats and donkeys, too. Sometimes they tamed birds, rats, and other captured animals, even a wild boar. A French air corps squadron of American expatriots sported an eye-catching pair of lion cubs as its mascots, nicknaming them Whiskey and Soda.

"People who haven't been at the front don't know what a little companionship means to a man on patrol duty, or in a dugout, or what a frisky pup means to a whole company," explained British Lieutenant Ralph Kynoch during the First World War. "The pups know when a barrage is on where they can find safety, and they go there, unless the man they look to as master is going somewhere else. Trust the dog to stick hard by no matter whether it is in the danger zone or not," he emphasized.

"If we can't get a dog we'll take a goat, or a cat, or a pig, a rabbit, a sheep, or, yes, even a wildcat," Kynoch had said. "We'll take anything for a trench companion—but give us a dog first."

★ CHAPTER THREE ★

SOMEWHERE IN FRANCE

THOUGHTS OF DEPARTURE AND COMBAT INEVITABLY GREW among the men at Camp Yale during the summer of 1917, and Stubby may well have sensed that change was afoot. Partings between soldiers and their visitors became more emotionally charged. The marching band stopped performing. The troops consolidated their belongings. Then it happened. On a mid-September evening, members of Conroy's regiment packed up their tents and loaded their backpacks. Next, under the cover of darkness, they began to march away from their temporary home on the Yale athletic fields.

Robert Conroy later wrote, "Stubby was sadly told it was useless to go any farther because dogs would not be permitted to board the ship." He added, with his trademark wit, "Stubby naturally could not understand that." But Stubby could see that his endless supply of free bones and table scraps was on the move, not to mention his best friend. So, in the dark of night, Stubby stepped into formation, marched with the men to the railway depot, and hopped aboard a train car bound for Newport News, Virginia.

No one tried to stop him.

The mobilization of the Yankee Division was one of the marvels of World War I. In a matter of months, Maj. Gen. Clarence R. Edwards and his staff had mustered and shipped to Europe a fighting force of 28,000 men. Just finding passage for that many individuals was a logistical nightmare, but the YD leadership had succeeded. Soldiers departed from Hoboken, New York City, Newport News, and Montreal. Some headed directly to France; others arrived by way of Great Britain. Some traveled on merchant ships that had been requisitioned for military transport; others shared rides on commercial liners alongside civilians. At journey's end, the YD became the first newly formed division of American troops to reach France; only the Army regulars of the First Division (nicknamed the Big Red One because of its insignia) had arrived earlier.

When Conroy reached Newport News, he faced a serious problem: What should he do with Stubby? Officers might have looked the other way in New Haven, or not noticed, when a stray dog took part in the chaotic nighttime boarding of a troop train. But a ship? Fat chance. Soldiers would be marching up a narrow gangplank. Someone's girlfriend would be easier to spirit on board than a cheerful dog.

Conroy, in a show of Yankee ingenuity, improvised. Rather than trying to smuggle the dog on board himself, he enlisted the aid of a crewmember from the *Minnesota,* the vessel designated for his passage to France. Prior to the ship's departure, the seaman quietly secured his stowaway in an engine room coal bin, and Stubby remained there until the boat was well out to sea. Then the two friends were reunited, and, remarkably, the dog's presence remained unchallenged. Their voyage lasted the better part of a month. Seasickness may have plagued other passengers on board the ship, but not Stubby. As one newspaper reporter later suggested, "Stubby's life was one soup bone after another," from then on.

*Stubby acquired plenty of military training during
the First World War, but he enjoyed just being a dog, too.
This undated photograph catches him after a swim.*

Typically the ships that departed from Newport News as part
of the mobilization effort served as livestock transports, carrying
the required military horses and mules to Europe. Plenty of these
animals got seasick, just like the humans, making such passages
noisy, messy, and filled with work. The *Minnesota*, however, was

tasked with transporting troops instead of livestock, and that made for an easier passage.

A certain amount of military routine persisted throughout the trip—including guard duty, which Stubby reportedly shared—but the men had plenty of free time, too. Those soldiers not leaning over the rails with seasickness passed the hours with card games, correspondence, reading, and conversation. Food varied in quality, but at least it came at predictable intervals. Some of these transport ships traveled alone, but more of them traveled in convoys and with military escorts as a protection against submarine attacks.

When the *Minnesota* reached France in early October, Conroy employed a more straightforward method for disembarking: He hoisted his pack, concealed Stubby in his overcoat, and carried him off the ship. His buddies, according to Conroy, provided "good interference," and the dog again escaped detection.

By this time Stubby's friends had made him a set of military ID tags. The idea of affixing a pair of durable identification tags on soldiers gained widespread use during the First World War as a way of naming and accounting for the dead. U.S. soldiers hung pairs of metal discs from their necks. Naturally, Stubby's tags hung from his leather collar. His tags read:

STUBBY
102nd INF
26th DIV

Ringing the central text was the name "J.R. Conroy" and the number "63254," Conroy's official service number. Even in that era such discs were nicknamed dog tags, and Conroy, with his rich sense of humor, must have enjoyed the joke.

The arriving Americans experienced the first of many instances of culture shock when they encountered the local form of military ground transportation. Doughboys quickly learned that the French moved combat troops not by passenger coach but by boxcar. They called their carriages "40 & 8s" because they could carry *40 hommes et 8 cheveaux,* that is, 40 men or, alternatively, 8 horses. The Americans nicknamed the boxcars "side-door Pullmans," a tongue-in-cheek reference to the luxurious railway cars from back home. If the occupants were lucky, their boxcar included some straw to cushion the floor. Weather permitting, soldiers traveled with the doors pushed back, seated in turns with their legs hanging outside the openings.

The 102nd did not linger long at the Atlantic coastal city of St. Nazaire. Instead, doughboys proceeded almost immediately from the city's port to its rail yard where, once the shock had worn off, the men climbed into the 40 & 8s. In Conroy and Stubby's case, their car became a 40 & 1s, as in *40 hommes et 1 chien.* The regiment's officers, per the local custom, rode in accompanying passenger cars. For the next few days, Conroy, Stubby, and their comrades remained confined to boxcars, except for brief breaks, while their train lumbered across northern France toward the war zone.

At some point soon after reaching Europe, the powers that be found out about Stubby. The story goes that, before Conroy or his furry friend could be reprimanded or punished, Stubby, by then a well-trained observer of military protocol, had sat back on his haunches, reared up from the ground, raised his right paw, and given the critical officer a doggy salute. That did it. Stubby was pronounced an official mascot for his unit, and he and Conroy were allowed to proceed without rebuke.

Conroy and his fellow doughboys did not begin fighting immediately, however. Plans called for American forces to gain seasoning at French training camps before assuming combat assignments. Artillery units headed to Brittany for instruction on firing the French artillery guns that were in use at the front. These outfits found themselves stationed southwest of Rennes at a French military camp called Coëtquidan. (The men authored a playful transliteration of the site's hard-to-decode spelling as "Quit your kidd'n.") Meanwhile, the 102nd and other infantry units from the Yankee Division headed toward Neufchâteau, a city in eastern France that is located southwest of Toul and Nancy.

General Edwards set up his command post in the city itself, and YD men were parceled out to prearranged shelters, scattered throughout the community and its neighboring towns. Officers might earn actual rooms in civilian homes or hotels; the rank

French children came out to watch and wave in the spring of 1918 when the 101st Ammunition Train of the Yankee Division passed through the town of Soulosse on its way to the front.

and file were not so lucky. Some were quartered in French-made barracks. Others bunked in barns, sheds, attics, storehouses, and stables. Accommodations ranged from simple to primitive, and almost all of them were unheated, at least in any meaningful way.

Where Conroy lived during this transition went unrecorded, but it seems safe to assume that whatever his circumstances, he felt a bit more at home because Stubby was nearby. The two of them, like everyone else, would have made the best of an Army that was still figuring out how to feed and shelter so many soldiers. When the supply system worked, the men obtained food from nearby Army storehouses, and, in those early days, they were often left to cook for themselves. When the system faltered, soldiers scrambled to fill in supply gaps on their own and scrounge for fuel. Some men became desperate enough to trade articles of clothing in exchange for cash or food, a swap that might have seemed good in the short run but created new problems later on when temperatures began to fall.

With General Edwards established in Neufchâteau, the Yankee Division's four infantry regiments set up their own command posts in proximity to their own troops, placing Conroy and Stubby at the hub of a growing network of interaction between the fighting units. Previously the infantry regiments had been scattered in camps throughout New England. By late October 1917, the YD infantrymen had all reached France, and they could begin to train together. Many only now had the opportunity to meet their division leader. General Edwards won the men's loyalty by respecting the local ties that bound their individual companies and battalions together. "Is all the family here tonight?" he reportedly liked to ask his men when making nighttime rounds through encamped troops.

Although some Yankee Division officers were career Army staffers, many of the men who guided YD companies and regiments were citizen-soldiers. Stateside they had been lawyers, doctors, and politicians. One had worked in insurance, another in the auto business, a third as a judge. Their leadership service in the National Guard had made them officers when they enlisted in the U.S. Army, even though they had not earned their military standing at West Point. The men under their command had looked up to their leaders at home, and they trusted them in the field. Edwards understood this. He knew such loyalty would be invaluable once the troops reached the front lines. The challenge was to sustain that Yankee spirit while preparing the men for the realities of trench warfare.

The Yankee Division embarked on a demanding, three-stage training program devised by General Pershing and his staff for arriving troops. Each phase involved greater and greater integration of the fighting forces until, by the end, it was imagined that an entire 28,000-man division would be practicing war games in open terrain. This training introduced the doughboys to instructors who represented their counterparts from England (generically nicknamed Tommy, or the Tommies) and France (called the *Poilu,* a cultural term of endearment that translates literally as "the hairy one"). Together they prepared to face their adversaries, especially the Germans, who were tagged with such pejoratives as Fritz, Huns, and the Boche.

Phase one of their European training looked to the Yankee soldiers an awful lot like what they had left behind in New England: marching and drilling without proper weaponry. Eventually, though, rifles arrived, along with grenades and machine guns, artillery pieces and shells. Adjusting to the resulting sights and sounds was probably a challenge for men and mascot alike. Nonetheless, the soldiers welcomed the chance to train with weapons at last. They worked on marksmanship, practiced the teamwork of firing heavy weaponry, and learned how to lob grenades. (British instructors promoted an underhanded cricket-style pitch that confounded the Americans; U.S. soldiers turned to their familiar sport of baseball for inspiration instead.) They labored six days a week for six hours a day, not counting routine military assignments such as guard duty or inspections.

Robert Conroy kept no known journal about his wartime service, and no letters home have passed down through the family, but news accounts after the war and general knowledge about the workings of the Army offer a broad idea of how he—and Stubby—served in France. As one reporter put it, "Stubby's history overseas is the story of almost any average doughboy." Conroy and his four-footed friend certainly traveled, slept, and ate like the rest of the infantrymen, and Conroy undoubtedly received training in trench warfare. Conroy, too, took his turns with guard duty; when he did, Stubby stood watch beside him.

Conroy's assignment to the regimental headquarters company, though, gave him a wider range of responsibilities than most men, and it offered him greater freedom of movement. One of his regular duties during the winter of 1917–18 was as a dispatch rider. Conroy, astride a horse, with Stubby trotting alongside, delivered messages between the regimental command post and General Edwards's headquarters at Neufchâteau, or to outlying units of the 102nd and their local trainers. This mobility allowed them to visit notable landmarks in the area, too, including Domrémy, the birthplace of French heroine Jeanne d'Arc. Local affection for Stubby prompted someone to give the dog a souvenir medal that honored the famed martyr, and it became Conroy's first treasured memento of his time with Stubby in France.

Frank P. Sibley, a reporter for the *Boston Globe* who spent the war embedded with the YD, published an early history of their experiences upon returning home. In *With the Yankee Division in France,* he describes one of the increasingly complex exercises that the soldiers practiced while stationed near Neufchâteau. After soldiers had dug a sample network of trenches, battalions took turns practicing offensive and defensive maneuvers around them. In place of artillery fire, Army buglers sounded long single notes of call. The musicians stood at fixed positions across the width of a battlefield and played their notes in concert with the advancing troops. Buglers stood silent until the troops aligned with them, and then fell silent again after they passed. This tandem work represented the artillery technique of a rolling barrage, where gun crews advanced in the wakes of infantrymen, firing cover shells toward enemy lines over the moving ranks of foot soldiers.

As Conroy explored the French countryside with Stubby and other service members, the men observed similarities and differences between it and home. Some recognized a familiar roll to the hills or traversed fields that could have stood in their home counties. Yet they encountered civilians dressed in unfamiliar styles of clothing who spoke a foreign language and lived with different customs, including the routine storage of barnyard manure adjacent to their residences. (Doughboys living near such dwellings industriously hauled the waste away, only to watch the piles accumulate again.)

One thing wholly new to the Americans, though, was French mud. "Real mud." "The worst sort of mud that I have ever become acquainted with." "Slippery yellow clay which hangs to your shoes and more and more keeps collecting." The mind-boggling French mud became a constant additional challenge for the soldiers, and they mailed countless descriptions of it to the folks back home. Military censors prohibited the inclusion of any identifying details of place or mission, so such epistles were simply attributed to having been sent from "somewhere in France."

The French weather offered doughboys plenty of options for complaint, and even locals judged the 1917–18 season as unusually severe. First came incessant fall rains: Hence the mud. Boots and clothing became caked in muck, and surely mud clung to Stubby's feet and fur, too. Eventually temperatures dropped to the point where the ground froze—a definite bright spot in terms of controlling the mud. But the cold temperatures persisted and were ever present in the men's lives, whether indoors or out, given the makeshift nature of their quarters and their lack of fuel. Now, instead of training in rain, the soldiers performed their maneuvers in wet snow, sleet, icy winds, even blizzards. Leather boots stayed perpetually wet and began to rot. Foot ailments became a serious concern, and few gifts from home were more welcomed than a pair of hand-knitted woolen socks.

As miserable as the men were, they still had music. The regimental marching bands that Stubby first heard in the States provided an ever present soundtrack to the scene in France, and songs from home ran through the soldiers' heads and poured out of their lips. It was an era when singing was a national pastime; even Conroy could contribute a decent baritone to a tune. Elsie Janis and other popular entertainers of the day toured France to amuse the troops. Official units of American soldiers were tasked with creating their own touring theatrical and musical reviews, too, and reportedly went on to perform even when shell fire threatened to disrupt their acts.

Naturally, when the nation went to war, its composers did, too—at least musically. George M. Cohan, Irving Berlin, and countless others penned lyrics and melodies that kept time moving on both sides of the Atlantic. Just the titles of the songs capture the spirit of the effort: "When Yankee Doodle Learns to 'Parlez-vous Française.' " "America, Here's My Boy." "If the Kaiser Were Wiser He'd Keep Far Away." "Just a Baby's Prayer at

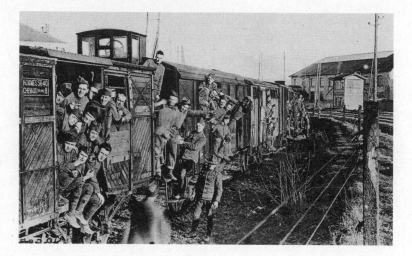

Members of the 101st Infantry Regiment and other Yankee Division doughboys piled into 40 & 8 boxcars when they departed Neufchâteau in February 1918, heading for the trenches.

Twilight (For Her Daddy Over There)." "Good-bye Broadway, Hello France."

Irving Berlin penned a silly song for sailors called "Over the Sea, Boys." His refrain of "Yo-Ho! Yo-Ho!" riffs through stanzas that end with such playful couplets as "We'll fill our guns with Navy beans / And shoot the German submarines," and "We have to leave our wives behind / For fighting of a different kind."

Newspaper headlines of America's entry into the war had inspired George M. Cohan to write "Over There," a bouncy march that became a runaway national hit:

> *Over there over there*
> *Send the word, send the word over there*
> *That the Yanks are coming the Yanks are coming*
> *The drums rum-tum-tumming everywhere . . .*

When Elsie Janis toured France to entertain the troops, she crafted an adaptation of Cohan's song, calling it "Over Here." She taught it to the men and together they would sing such lines as, "Mother dear, dry that tear / Soon your worries will all disappear," because, as her song went, the American troops would secure a victory.

In early February 1918, the Yankee Division received orders to move closer to the front for its next phase of training. Conroy and Stubby were once again on the move. As the soldiers climbed into transport trucks and 40 & 8 boxcars, groups of men broke into song. Perhaps Conroy joined in. Maybe some of them, too, sang some of Cohan's original lyrics: "The Yanks are coming, the Yanks are coming," the men may have bellowed, ending with the roaring pledge "And we won't come back till it's over over there."

CHAPTER FOUR

IN AND OUT OF THE TRENCHES

DURING 1917, WHILE AMERICANS PREPARED FOR THEIR country to enter the Great War, Russian citizens wanted to drop out of the conflict. As Conroy enlisted in the National Guard, while Stubby wandered into Camp Yale, and as General Pershing plotted military strategy with his Allied counterparts, a pair of revolutions swept across Russia. Supply shortages and mounting casualties in the fight with Germany contributed to the unrest that ended the reign of Czar Nicholas II and ushered in the rise of Bolshevik leader Vladimir Lenin. Lenin had no interest in sustained combat with Germany, and by March 1918 the two nations had signed a peace treaty. This development provided German military commanders with their hoped-for windfall. With the guns now silent on its eastern front, they could transfer newly idle German troops—some one million men—to fight against the Allies on its western front.

Many of these soldiers received extra training and equipment as part of their redeployment. They practiced a new way of fighting, one designed to break through the entrenched battle lines across Belgium and France. Armed with machine guns and flame-throwers, among other weapons, they were assigned to infiltrate weak points in the Allied defenses. Next, these elite fighters would press deep into enemy territory and expose the remaining fortifications to attack from the conventional infantrymen who followed behind them. Military leaders called these soldiers *Stosstruppen*—storm troopers. The one-two punch delivered by these paired forces was designed to create chaos, panic, and defeat. The Germans planned to begin deploying the troops in the spring of 1918.

Conroy's Yankee Division and other American outfits raced to get ready for the anticipated spring offensive. Moving all the men and matériel toward the front lines represented a logistical challenge that was met with a mix of ingenuity and hard work. Keeping the fighting forces supplied became as crucial to the war's outcome as the performance of the fighters themselves. Gun crews practiced loading and unloading ammunition trains stocked with artillery pieces and shells. An effort that might have taken more than two hours on the first attempt shrank to as little as 15 minutes after months of practice in advance and at the front.

The Army's Quartermaster Corps perfected the procurement and distribution of food, the repair and replacement of clothing, and the transport of other supplies in an unfamiliar country where its residents spoke an unknown language. This corps managed warehouses full of stores near railway hubs, and they coordinated the distribution of goods to the places where they were needed. That work required the shipment of countless vehicle tires, boxcars full of animal forage, and train cars loaded with ammunition shells, among other items. Such movements were not without dangers, even at some distance from the front lines. In the dawning era of aerial combat, one never knew when enemy planes might conduct a scouting mission or hostile raid, so the trains included machine guns and gunners tasked with defending cargo.

Although the Yankee Division infantrymen shipped out from Neufchâteau via train and truck, they completed their journeys on foot (probably someone's idea of how to give the men further conditioning). Conroy would have joined his fellow soldiers in the trek, and Stubby appears to have kept up without complaint. Each soldier bore responsibility for carrying his own gear. Stubby caught a pass on that duty, however; his two-legged friends carried everything from spare clothing to toiletries, from weaponry to ammunition, from food rations to eating utensils and dishes. It didn't take long before the men learned to travel light. Items of sentimental value and personal comfort had to be very dear indeed to merit the effort it took to haul them on long marches. Machine-gunners often found themselves toting not only their personal gear but some or all of a machine gun (with each weapon weighing in at more than 100 pounds, including the tripod).

Early in 1918, the 102nd Regiment gained a new commander, Col. John H. Parker. This career officer and veteran of the Spanish-American War had earned the nicknames "Gatling Gun" Parker and "Machine Gun" Parker because of his acknowledged expertise in the usage of rapid-firing weapons. The men liked their new commander from the start. The assignment of a new leader to the regiment meant that Stubby had to charm a new commanding officer, which he apparently promptly did. It was later reported that "Stubby was the only member of Parker's regiment that could talk back to him and get away with it." Parker saw no reason to question the animal's role as the 102nd's mascot, and he gave Conroy permission to advance with him toward the combat zone. They reached their new posting on February 5.

The men and their mascot found themselves at battle positions along a relatively quiet stretch of the western front named after the Chemin des Dames, a notable highway that traversed part of the territory. For the first time, the entire Yankee Division—artillery included—was stationed together; thus united, the division would participate in phase two of its training. Its various regiments and batteries were assigned to spend a month shadowing and serving alongside their compatriots from XI Corps of the French Army. The division's American commanders collaborated with their French counterparts in the maneuvers and retained overall responsibility for their own men.

Conroy, Stubby, and the other soldiers took up residence in an underground network of bunkers that had been fashioned out of former limestone quarries. Wooden planking covered the walls and floors of many of the subterranean tunnels and chambers. Soldiers slept in bunk beds covered with chicken wire and straw. Underground passageways connected the living and sleeping quarters. Some of the rooms lay 30 or more feet below ground, and they offered the men a refuge of comparative quiet and safety from the combat activities taking place outside.

Conroy's duties expanded upon reaching the front lines when he was assigned to the intelligence unit of the regimental headquarters company, tasked with observing enemy troop movements. Among other reconnaissance, the work would have taken him—and, presumably, Stubby—through the bands of defensive trenches and their connecting communication links in search of eyewitness reports from the front lines. Conroy's freedom of movement would have introduced Stubby to many of the regiment's men, adding to the mascot's profile within the corps.

Meanwhile, the regiment's infantrymen rotated in and out of the lines of combat trenches, defending the front lines against periodic enemy raids. Most of the action, though, came from perpetual bombardments of artillery fire. The Americans became adept at recognizing the distinctive sounds and behaviors of enemy and Allied fire. Artillery guns of different calibers corresponded to the size of the shells that they fired. The various French field guns, which A.E.F. batteries used as well, discharged shells in a range of sizes, including 75 mm, 105 mm, and 155 mm. (Different batteries received different calibers of guns, so artillery units typically had personal experience with only some of this range of equipment.)

Allies also used giant battleship guns—known, too, as railway guns because they were transported on the ground using rail lines; the enormous weapons fired shells almost twice the size of the largest field artillery piece and had a range of many miles. These guns emitted a predictable giant booming sound when

Armed forces relied on a primitive system of hastily strung telephone wires for much of their battlefront communication. This photo shows a soldier laying line for the 101st Field Signal Battalion of the Yankee Division during the fall of 1918.

fired; the others made noises ranging from rapid-firing barks to deeper roars.

German artillery came with its own telltale soundtrack. The German naval/railway gun fired 210 mm shells that delivered a powerful percussive as well as destructive force. Assorted German *minenwerfers*, nicknamed minnies, launched trench mortars of varying calibers, including one as large as 50 pounds. A trademark "plop" sounded with the launch of one of these shells, and soldiers scrambled to avoid its plodding trajectory. The 88-mm "whiz-bangs," in contrast, traveled faster than the speed of sound. Allied troops had a saying that "you never hear the shell that's going to get you," and it is easy to imagine how one of these "whiz-bangs" could catch a man unawares. The men who survived the shell's impact then had to endure the delayed arrival of its volley of sound.

Soldiers on both sides stacked artillery shells like cord wood and launched them by the hundreds. Guns might fall quiet for a time only to renew their dialogues in response to a probing volley from the opposite side. Just keeping these remote gun crews supplied with ammunition was one more logistical challenge for the war effort. Supply crews employed every possible means of conveyance to move shells to the front, including horse-drawn wagons and carts pulled by dogs. Such operations often took place at night to reduce the chance of being targeted by enemy fire, but that meant navigating a darkened landscape pockmarked with the impact craters from earlier rounds of shelling.

The warfront landscape appeared just as surreal in daylight. Tangles of barbed wire secured various defenses. Charred skeletons represented former trees. The land's most productive crop became shallow graves with makeshift markers. Nearby villages stood in ruins, often abandoned by their residents. Add the lingering odors of exploded shells, the smell of excrement from horses and other livestock (not to mention humans), the ground tremors caused each time a large gun was fired, the percussive force of falling enemy shells, and one can begin to imagine the background scene that greeted the Yankee Division when it reached what was actually regarded as a quiet part of the western front.

How Stubby reacted to gunfire and artillery bombardments was later reported with a healthy dose of dramatic license. News accounts claim, variously, that Stubby "never once winced under fire" (per a 1925 article in the *Washington Post*); that he combined an "angry howl [with a] mad canter from one part of the lines to the other" (*New York Times,* from 1926); that "every artillery barrage left poor, forsaken Stubby quivering and shaking on all four legs" (*Hartford Courant,* 1919); or that, conversely (as reported in the *Hartford Courant* five days after its previous story), "in the tradition of the Yankee Division . . . he never yelped." Truth be told, Stubby probably did all of the above and more as the war unfolded.

On March 17, 1918, the members of the YD experienced their first exposure to poisonous gas. By that point in the war the Germans had employed three different kinds of gas in combat: chlorine, phosgene, and the now infamous mustard gas. On the 17th, shells carrying one of these toxins fell on the soldiers for hours at a time. The men had trained for such a situation, and each soldier had his own gas mask for personal defense. Stubby had one, too, thanks to Conroy and a sympathetic Allied officer.

Initially Conroy had ordered a French-made doggy gas mask for his friend, but the device did not conform securely enough to the animal's head. So a French lieutenant fashioned an alternative mask for the popular mascot using military supplies, and Conroy trained Stubby to put up with wearing it. With Conroy's coaching, the dog learned to retreat to his dugout bunker during a gas bombardment.

Before long Stubby, using his canine-keen sense of smell (and probably his hearing, too), began to recognize an impending gas attack. Then he'd alert his comrades by barking an alarm and, when necessary, nipping at sleeping soldiers. Stubby's alert then helped trigger the standard bells of warning for an attack and allowed everyone, himself included, to be more prepared when the gas shells began to fall.

On one occasion, the alert dog happened upon a soldier who was sleeping below ground in a dugout and had not heard the topside alarm. Stubby stirred him awake, saving him from serious injury since gas regularly settled in the underground network of tunnels and chambers. Later on, the grateful sergeant, John J. Curtin, composed a poem in tribute to Stubby: "Listen to me and I will tell / Of a dog who went all through hell," Curtin began. His multistanza tribute included the couplet: "He always knew when to duck the shells / And buried his nose at the first gas smells."

Conroy recorded a tantalizingly brief accounting of Stubby's wartime experiences. He explained that, during combat duty, "Stubby was always on his own—he was never tied up anywhere—he seemed to know that no one could bother with him during action and that he had to stay quietly under cover if he expected to remain a live mascot." At times, Stubby reportedly took advantage of his freedom of movement to go, as is said in the military, AWOL, or absent without leave. Most of these disappearances were brief, and, as reporters later joked, "he always came in clean and sober," and he "never once spent time in the brig."

On one occasion, though, the dog went missing for much longer than usual, and "the division mourned him as lost." Then, by chance, a soldier from the YD's 101st Infantry Regiment spotted a familiar-looking animal during an interaction with a French infantry unit. There was Stubby, being led on a leash by a French *Poilu!* The doughboy challenged his counterpart and demanded that he surrender Stubby so he could be returned to his original outfit. The man refused. The Yankee soldier grew more insistent and began to threaten the Frenchman with disciplinary action. With reluctance the *Poilu* relented, and the American, taking custody of the popular mascot, returned him to Conroy.

Stubby's popularity came from his personality. He befriended his fellow doughboys by sharing time with them. He kept men company while they stood watch. He snuggled alongside napping men. His relentless good humor lifted the spirits of soldiers anxiously waiting in front-line trenches, and he had a dog's knack for knowing when someone needed the comfort of an uncomplaining companion. "He was not a 'one man' dog, but everyone's friend," explained a news reporter after the war. Stubby charmed one and all, from the Yankee Division's commander on down, "but his intimate friends were the mud-bespattered doughboys in the front lines," wrote the journalist.

Infantrymen rotated in and out of the front-line trenches, retreating when they weren't on duty to the relative quiet and safety of the underground quarters located a short distance from their defensive lines. This split service created an odd blending of mundane downtime with life-or-death intensity. Soldiers began to adapt to the contrasts and filled their lulls with simple pleasures—playing poker, writing home, reading, drawing, and so on, not to mention hanging out with Stubby.

Plus the men had personal chores to do, from washing out socks to mending torn clothing to dealing with matters of individual hygiene. The latter quickly became a rather hopeless pursuit. Soldiers soon abandoned hope of having dependable access to showers, or even the chance to wash up. Who knew when they'd ever receive a set of fresh clothing? As a result, even though the men may have cursed the Kaiser and hurled insults at the Huns, they lived closer still to their number one personal enemy: lice.

The body lice, which the men routinely referred to as cooties, were omnipresent on the front. They thrived on human blood and luxuriated in the dirty, closely quartered environment of trench life. Stubby would have been untroubled by the lice because the parasite's diet was restricted to people. For the mascot's dough-boy pals, though, living in the trenches and living with cooties became synonymous states of being.

The soldiers employed a variety of methods to combat the itchy, nipping bugs—from boiling their underclothing to method-ically picking the lice off of garments (a pastime playfully nick-named "reading" clothes)—but none of these techniques worked for long. "I sometimes wonder whether my shirt belongs to me or to them," observed one YD soldier when writing home about the lice, "but we get used to them after a while."

The U.S. Army added its weight to the fight with roving disin-fecting squads that periodically met up with the men, particularly when the soldiers were being relieved from front-line service. In these instances, soldiers stripped bare and turned their clothes over for inspection. Those items in need of repair or replace-ment were set aside; usable clothing headed to the portable laundry machine. This device treated the garments with a cootie-unfriendly combination of pressurization and hot steam. Lice killed, the clean clothes were then hung to dry. Meanwhile the soldiers flocked to portable showers. Most of these facilities were primitive outdoor devices that simply relied on gravity to force water through a network of pipes and shower nozzles.

Army staff photographers dutifully documented the laundry and shower systems along with every other aspect of the war. One captioned album of these photos contains such cheerful comments as: "Note the happy appearance of these men as they are about to leave the plant," and "They are going home as merry as small boys from a school picnic." Instead of smelling as fresh as a daisy, though, clean soldiers smelled like creosote, having applied a smoky distillation of the chemical substance to their bodies. With luck, the aftershave-like solution would act as a temporary deterrent to reinfestation.

Stubby may have earned a pass on body lice, but humans and dogs alike battled perpetually with rats. Trench rats thrived in the dirty, crowded conditions at the warfront. They grew enormous—as large as house cats—as they scrounged fearlessly through the subterranean passageways and chambers at the front. Soldiers described seeing "green eyes about everywhere," after extinguishing their lights. The men learned to sleep through the animals' nighttime visits, even when the rodents ran over the top of their bodies.

The rats, like the lice, could spread diseases, so soldiers tried to fight this enemy, too. One strategy involved employing dogs with a natural penchant for killing rats. These so-called ratters offered some control of the varmints, but rats remained as omnipresent as lice throughout the war. Stubby's terrier genes made him a good rat hunter, too, so he added rat patrol to his growing list of wartime duties. Did Stubby eat the rats he caught? Quite possibly. He may have hunted for other wild game, too. Most of all, though, he probably continued to rely on his military buddies for food.

It fell to the Army's Quartermaster Corps to procure and distribute the provisions required to literally feed an army. Purchasers bought local beef by the side, potatoes by the cartload, and cabbages by the sackful. The French employed similar methods but included another staple in their soldiers' diet—red wine—which they purchased in casks so large that two of them would fill a standard flatbed railcar. Quartermasters supplied the troops with crates of cigarettes and tobacco, too, selling these items to the men via traveling commissary stores. Alternatively, the men turned to social welfare outfits—such as the YMCA, Salvation

Army, Jewish Welfare Board, and so on—for cigarettes, candy, cups of hot cocoa, doughnuts, and other treats.

When troops were on the move, their accompanying field kitchens could remain operational in transit, pulled along by mules or horses, smoke and all. Otherwise cooks set up camp far enough from the front so that their noise wouldn't draw direct fire, but close enough so that the food could feasibly reach the troops. The resulting proximity to the war zone assured that stray artillery shells periodically became an added chef's challenge. The cooked food was transported to the trenches in semi-insulated ceramic containers, but it rarely arrived hot

Soldiers learned to make a meal in just about any setting while serving in the trenches. A group of doughboys from the 102nd Infantry Regiment shared this communal repast during March 1918.

because it could take an hour or more to cover the distance between cook and combat.

Twice daily, small parties of men were dispatched from the trenches to travel to camp and collect rations for their platoons. Sometimes animals helped carry the loads. Stealth played a role in successful food delivery since any obvious movement invited enemy fire. Extreme measures were taken—even slitting a donkey's nostrils to prevent braying, for example—to assure that animals and clanging pans didn't expose the travelers to machine-gun fire or shelling.

Otherwise, little suspense accompanied the arrival of the daily chow. Doughboys endured a monotonous diet of canned corned beef, other tinned meat, bacon, and various permutations of stew. They nicknamed the first dish "corned willy" and called the latter "slumgullion" or "slum." French canned meat became known as "monkey meat." Local potatoes, turnips, celery, and other vegetables livened things up at times, as did the local bread, "big, round loaves made from whole wheat, very nutritious and welcome to a hungry man," as one soldier later described it. Stubby, when he wanted to supplement the morsels shared by Conroy and other soldiers, probably knew just where to find the cooks who would be willing to throw him a bone, or better.

During periods of intense shelling, the kitchens gave up cooking and sent field rations to the men—preserved or semiperishable foods such as canned sardines, cold cuts of meat, and instant coffee. These stores arrived in sealed metal containers (rat- and rainproof) that could sustain a designated group of men for four days at a time. Whether they ate fresh food or canned rations, the soldiers craved chocolate and other sweets; mostly they relied on packages from home to satisfy those tastes.

Conroy, Stubby, and the rest of the Yankee Division spent six weeks stationed alongside their French mentors near the

Chemin des Dames, literally learning what it meant to be in the trenches. But before the Americans could undertake their final phase of training—joint military exercises with the United States Army's 42nd Division—they found themselves on their own, transferred to more intense duty, their training suspended. The German spring offensive had begun, and its troops were penetrating established Allied lines. Training or no training, the time had come for U.S. soldiers to test their might. Could they turn the tide of war?

A domino-like reshuffling of troops began. General Pershing dispatched the U.S. First Division, which had completed its entire training program, to a hot spot near the French town of Cantigny. The Big Red One went on to gain infamous distinction in the ensuing bloody battle to retake and hold the town. Meanwhile, Conroy and his fellow soldiers were transported to fill the trenches being vacated by the First Division near Toul. The Yankee Division men had trained along the Chemin des Dames in the shadows of their French counterparts, practicing the basics of combat under this local guidance; in the Toul sector, they were assigned to defend territory on their own. From then on, the accelerating pace of the war assured that no other U.S. divisions (beyond the First) would complete the program of training originally envisioned for arriving troops.

Commanders for the 26th Division parceled out their forces to defend, as best they could, battle lines nearly 12 miles in length that had previously been guarded by both an American division and one of the typically smaller French ones. Spreading the 28,000-man force proportionally meant that fewer than 2,500 men covered each mile's multiple bands of interconnected (and thus hard to defend) trenches. Fortunately the sector at least was considered a "quiet" one, subject only to routine artillery fire and periodic raids. It was, in fact, a place where divisions were historically sent to "rest" after having served in more stressful battle zones.

The Yankee Division's duty there did not begin quietly, however. Although the relief of the First Division had been ordered to take place in secrecy, the Germans weren't fooled. April showers—of rain and shells—challenged the men as they settled into their duties. Some soldiers reached the front, looked across No Man's Land toward the German trenches, and could see signs posted by the enemy that read, with chilling sarcasm, "Welcome 26th Division."

The headquarters company for the 102nd set up its base in a small French village north of Toul named Beaumont, putting them not even two miles from the front lines. By the third of April, all the American troops were in place, and the rotation of shifts of doughboys into and out of the trenches had begun. Did Conroy take his turn in the trenches with Stubby? Maybe not on a routine basis, given his primary responsibilities through the headquarters company, but he almost certainly would have visited the tangled web of interconnecting passages to deliver dispatches, and he may well have stood on guard there, too. When not on duty, Stubby and Conroy bunked with other soldiers in an underground dugout near the Beaumont headquarters.

Other members of Conroy's 102nd Regiment were on duty during the predawn hours of April 20, when the Germans began shelling a front-line fortification known as the Sibille trench. About 350 men from Companies C and D of the regiment's First Battalion had only just assumed responsibility for its defense when the intense barrage of artillery and poisonous gas began. The shelling coincided with a particularly rotten night of rainy weather, and it caught those on the receiving end at a moment of added vulnerability: This was their first night in the Sibille trench, and they were still familiarizing themselves with the layout of its defenses when the bombardment began.

Around 5:30 a.m., some two and a half hours after commencing fire, the Germans stopped. This turn of events brought no comfort, for, as the men knew from their training, it often meant that enemy troops were preparing to enter the artillery-softened zone. An opaque fog, laced with smoke and gas, now hung over the territory, adding further advantage to the attackers. Then, at various points along the trench, groups of German *Stosstruppen* materialized out of the mist. The Americans immediately had to wonder: Was this an ordinary raid, designed to disrupt defenses and capture prisoners? Or was some larger maneuver under way?

A fellow soldier sketched Robert Conroy as he relaxed in his bunk while stationed in Beaumont, France, during the spring of 1918. Stubby rests near his friend's feet, nestled in bedding (just right of the center crease of the drawing).

Not surprisingly, the intense German artillery barrage had severed the communication lines between field units and the rear command posts, leaving military tacticians with only the vaguest sense of what was transpiring along the front lines. In cases such as these, soldiers resorted to word-of-mouth and written communications instead. Because the Americans had no trained canine corps, they relied on human runners to carry such messages. These couriers, who sometimes traveled in pairs as a form of grim redundancy, left the comparative safety of their assigned posts and raced across open territory to convey battlefield reports and military orders. Such messengers were plucked from random duties—infantryman, auto mechanic, machine-gunner—because of their natural speed. That morning the battle zone descended into chaos so quickly, though, that reports were sporadic at best and hard to verify.

Companies C and D mustered a hearty defense of the Sibille trench, but they were outnumbered some six to one, and, despite heroic combat, they could not repulse their attackers. Many doughboys fought to the death rather than submit to capture. Having overrun the Sibille trench, the *Stosstruppen* advanced toward the next Allied fortifications, including the adjacent town of Seicheprey. The remains of this battle-scarred hamlet served as the headquarters for the commander of the regiment's First Battalion. When the Germans arrived, all the Americans joined in the defense of the territory, including a company cook who wielded a meat cleaver to deadly effect. The Germans, whose intentions had been to seize prisoners, not to hold territory, elected to withdraw rather than face such intense hand-to-hand combat.

Rumors flew throughout the conflict: Everyone in the Sibille trench was dead; the Germans were still in Seicheprey; the Germans planned to capture a vital road corridor inside Allied territory. "There was too much racket to think," one wounded man later observed, after he had crawled through machine-gun-fire toward a medical station. The misinformation led to miscalculations, including the raining of friendly artillery fire on the Americans who had survived the attack on Seicheprey. Only the arrival of an intrepid runner at the gun batteries straightened out that mix-up.

As news of the fight reached Colonel Parker back at the 102nd's headquarters post in Beaumont, he ordered all hands into action. No one yet knew the attackers' intentions. If the Germans were conducting more than a raid, he wanted to make sure the enemy breached no further trenches. Conroy grabbed his gun and, accompanied by Stubby, headed out to help reinforce the next line of defense. The high alert continued for hours.

Communication remained poor, but it eventually became clear that the Germans were in retreat. As they reversed direction, the Germans occupied the Sibille trench once again, this time pivoting so that they used it in a defensive position, taking cover there as they fired on pursuing doughboys. When the gun batteries learned of this development, they began shelling the Germans in the Sibille trench. Surviving Germans continued their retreat under fire, forcing their new prisoners to not only retreat with them but also help carry wounded American and German soldiers from the battlefield.

Conroy and Stubby remained on duty in the trenches through the hours of shelling and crossfire that followed the early-morning attack. That afternoon, as the fight seemed to wane, Stubby climbed to ground level and began to explore the forward territory. Then an unexpected enemy shell exploded near the exposed dog, and Stubby gave "a low howl of pain." When Conroy crawled out to help his friend, he discovered that Stubby had been hit by shrapnel in his breast and left foreleg. The soldier returned with the dog to the relative safety of their trench and administered first aid as best he could. Before long, the threat of attack really had passed, and Conroy was called back with his fellow soldiers to their headquarters in Beaumont.

Conroy entered the village carrying Stubby in his arms. A doctor at an Army first aid station saw the pair and called Conroy over so he could examine the mascot's wounds. Stubby's injuries were significant but not hopeless, he concluded, and he dressed them again. Then he ordered Conroy to place his friend alongside other wounded in a waiting ambulance. The ambulance was bound for a nearby field hospital, and the doctor knew that surgeons there could properly clean out and stitch up the dog's injuries. That the animal would even receive such notice, particularly on what was arguably the gravest day of fighting yet seen by the Yankee Division, attests to the popularity of the mascot within his regiment and beyond. "For days there was deep gloom in the outfit lest 'Stubby' should not get well," a newspaper account later claimed. Conroy undoubtedly worried about his companion. Spirits surely lifted when word came that the dog would recover.

By the time of the battle of Seicheprey, as it came to be known, a year had passed since Woodrow Wilson's call to arms. The men of the YD had weathered almost three months of combat duty by this point, and they understood, in a way that only war's eyewitnesses really can, the full weight of the expression "War is hell." The soldiers who did the best in this war zone, as in others, were the ones who adapted to the unnatural scene. The war became their job, and they stuck with it the way they had stuck with unpleasant work at home. Wet feet, ever present shelling, cold food, rats, lice, and the constant fear of calamity became a way of life. Thoughts of home, a sense of duty, the camaraderie of fellow soldiers served as tonics for the hardships. Robert Conroy had an added ally in the fight: Stubby.

Conroy later described Stubby as his "closest companion . . . during the war." Almost a century after his service, the soldier's eldest grandson, Curtis Deane, recalls that his grandfather was "very quiet" about what he did during the war. "He would just say, 'I was with Stubby.' " Deane notes that their bond went deeper than mere companionship. "Their relationship was seamless. They were one." Deane adds: "I have to tell you, that man was devoted to that dog," adding, "The dog may have been what got him through the war."

★ CHAPTER FIVE ★

SUMMER CAMPAIGNS

I T TOOK MORE THAN A MONTH FOR STUBBY TO FULLY RECOVER from his wounds. But, "like the proverbial cat," Robert Conroy later wrote, Stubby "seemed to have many lives." By the time the mascot returned to duty in early June, things were looking up for the Yankee Division. True, almost 200 Americans had been captured by the Germans during the raid of the Sibille trench, but casualties from the day's fighting, which became known as the battle of Seicheprey, were not as high as originally feared. Furthermore, the Germans, who had suffered 300 or more casualties in the exchange, seemed reluctant to tangle unnecessarily with the tenacious fighters of the 26th Division; they had barely challenged their American neighbors since the engagement on April 20. Plus the weather had turned at last. For almost the first time since reaching France, the Yankee Division doughboys could enjoy living outdoors.

A series of surviving photographs attests to the fine weather—and to the bond that had grown between Conroy and Stubby. At some point, perhaps as early as 1918, Conroy purchased a leather-bound scrapbook and began documenting his friend's life. He eventually glued a collection of five photographs onto one of the album's oversize black leaves and added a white-inked caption in his graceful penmanship at the bottom of the page. "Stubby at Beaumont France," it read. In one of the five sepia-toned prints, viewers see Stubby with a hangdog expression, head cocked to one side, ears up, tongue hanging out, as he studies the photographer who has gotten down to eye level to snap the picture.

There's a photo of Stubby seated on the hood of an ambulance, his head turned toward the three soldiers perched behind the dashboard. Conroy stands beside the dog and one wonders, Could this be the ambulance crew that transported the wounded mascot to the hospital? The answer is impossible to know. Another image captures Stubby standing on his hind legs, his front ones grasped by Conroy on one side and an unidentified pipe-toting fellow doughboy on the other. The stranger could be one of any 1,000 soldiers whom Stubby had befriended.

Conroy and Stubby pose alone in the remaining pair of photos. In one, Conroy crouches down and has scooped Stubby up so that the animal sits on his bent leg. The man's right arm encircles the dog's shoulder in the same sort of securing grip that a human might use when posing with a close friend. Stubby's head is level with his companion's, but his gaze is focused on an off-camera distraction. Conroy beams at the lens.

There is nothing posed about the final image. It's as if the photographer clicked the shutter during one of those random moments before or after the posing of a shot. It's a sunny day. Conroy, standing beneath a large tree, looks down at Stubby who has reared back on his hind legs so that he can rest his front paws on Conroy's left thigh. Stubby's head is upturned, his eyes locked on Conroy's downward gaze. The image captures the essence of their bond, such a natural fit of friendship, trust, and unconditional love. Conroy's military uniform and the Army truck parked in the photo's background attest to the fact that a war is going on around the pair, but such details seem inconsequential. The frozen moment embodies the sentiment of Conroy's grandson: Stubby and Conroy were one.

Stubby was back in fine form, having fully recovered from his April 20 shrapnel wound, when he rejoined Robert Conroy near the front lines in early June 1918.

The war hadn't gone away, though. Life in the Toul sector may have remained quiet, for a war zone, but there were still periodic raids across No Man's Land, artillery batteries still exchanged fire, and soldiers continued to live in that mental zone where what is, is—until it's not. Then, in late June, rumors began to circulate that the men had earned a break: They would receive furloughs; they were headed to Paris; they'd been asked to march in a Fourth of July parade. *Hooray!* After spending the better part of five months in the trenches, any or all of such options sounded better than staying in place.

The rumors took on the ring of truth when, soon after, the division was ordered out of the trenches and sent to a rail yard. Soldiers piled enthusiastically into 40 & 8s on a train headed toward Paris. *Fantastic!* Bystanders waved and cheered at the doughboys throughout the trip, and the men "shouted back until they were hoarse." When at last the Eiffel Tower appeared in the distance, excitement swelled among the men. All their anticipation evaporated, however, when the travelers felt their railcars being shunted onto an alternate set of tracks. Instead of continuing toward the French capital, this rail line led back toward the battlefront. Local residents still waved and cheered as the troops passed by, "but the boys had nothing left for response but a sad wave of the hand."

With that, Conroy, Stubby, and the rest of the Yankee Division moved from the relative quiet of the Toul sector to a much hotter front: the Marne. This region east of Paris, bisected by the Marne River, had hosted the first battle of the Marne in the opening months of the war. In late May 1918, the Germans began trying once again to push through the Allied defenses toward Paris. Fighting had already raged for more than a month by the time the YD arrived on the scene. At great cost, Marines from the Second Division had retaken some of the land lost during the initial

German assault. Now the 26th Division was tasked with defending the gains and preparing for further attacks.

The men didn't have long to wait. On July 15 the Germans tried again to crash through the Allied lines along the extensive front. They failed. The war's duration had begun to take its toll, both on the German front lines and back at home. A successful Allied naval blockade was hampering Germany's ability to feed its citizens, and the ranks of its army contained fewer and fewer able-bodied and experienced fighters. Meanwhile, each month hundreds of thousands of U.S. troops had begun landing in Europe. The Allies' increasingly well-fortified defenses, including the addition of the Yankee Division outside Château-Thierry, were becoming impenetrable. By July 17 the Germans had abandoned their assault.

The tide of the war was turning, and the Allies took the offensive starting on July 18. Working in concert, multiple divisions of French and American soldiers began to press eastward against the German lines; meanwhile, the German forces began an organized retreat, relinquishing land, but at the price of high Allied casualties, using the time created by combat delays to salvage matériel and men for later use in its defense. In reply, the Allies tried to squeeze the Germans into a tighter and tighter wedge of territory, hoping to capture prisoners and hardware as they progressed.

Conroy's responsibilities shifted with the change from defensive to offensive fighting. Now he helped to track the direction and nature of the German retreat, transmitting that intelligence back to command posts himself or via other messengers. Such information helped to inform military leaders as they plotted how best to pursue and intercept the retreating forces. Whether or not Stubby accompanied Conroy during such work went unrecorded, but the dog had to keep up with someone during the constantly shifting battlefront, and it seems likely that he hung close by Conroy during at least some of this reconnaissance work.

Yard by yard, and eventually mile by mile, the Allies pressed onward. Gone were the trenches of the Toul sector. Much of this fighting took place in the open, across fields of ripened wheat. The lack of cover exposed the advancing soldiers to horrendous machine-gun fire and left them with few places to shelter during artillery bombardments.

Making matters worse, the movements of infantrymen on the ever shifting battleground frequently outpaced those of artillery units. Ideally the artillery was supposed to operate as a sort of rolling barrage, delivering rounds of fire on enemy positions and thus softening up the territory that the infantry would proceed to seize. Then the artillery would advance, and the one-two maneuver would repeat itself. But as the pace of the advance quickened and the battlefields became cratered from waves of shelling, the artillery units found it hard to keep up.

The Allied offensive continued night and day. Soldiers discarded gear as they maneuvered in the summer heat, only to find themselves without shelter or cover during the odd moments when they were allowed to rest. The rolling kitchen wagons frequently fell behind in their pursuit of the troops, leaving the doughboys to subsist on emergency rations of hardtack.

The switch from defensive to offensive fighting exposed the Allied soldiers to a new measure of their progress: dead bodies. Their maneuvers netted them plenty of live ones, too, in the form of German prisoners of war. Meanwhile, fallen Allied comrades joined the landscape of mayhem, cut down by relentless rounds of machine-gun fire and shelling. At its worst, the fighting deteriorated into life-and-death struggles of hand-to-hand combat.

The capture of German soldiers and the wounding of American ones created new ways for Stubby to serve the war effort:

He became a rescue dog. How much training he underwent is unknown, but in short order the seasoned mascot proved adept at finding and comforting wounded men. He, as with other rescue dogs, learned to bypass German soldiers in favor of Allied ones. His ability to sniff out surviving humans whose presence might be obscured by waves of golden wheat made him particularly useful to the humans he assisted.

When Stubby found a soldier, he would either remain with him until help arrived or return to fetch the medics. If someone was dying, Stubby offered companionship so that the man would not die alone. Such work went on regardless of battlefield conditions. Thus, the already stressful task of hunting for and rescuing wounded men could become complicated by the added danger of dodging artillery shells. Fallen soldiers might languish for hours awaiting care. The lucky ones progressed up the chain of care, as needed, from battlefield aid stations to mobile field hospitals to established military hospitals.

Casualties mounted during the Allies' aggressive pursuit of the retreating Germans. For example, staff members at the American Red Cross Hospital in Neuilly-sur-Seine, just outside Paris, scrambled to accommodate the waves of wounded soldiers arriving from the summer offensive. After they ran out of beds, orderlies lined the corridors with patients resting on stretchers. Eventually more beds were found, but the men remained housed in hallways because there weren't enough wards to accommodate them all.

Newspapers back home reprinted the government's casualty lists, tallying them under headlines such as this accounting published August 8, 1918, in the *Hartford Courant*: "1,014 Casualties in Latest Lists—Total Shows 150 Killed in Action and 457 Wounded Severely . . . Few Connecticut Names." One can imagine the families and friends who scanned each new list, always grateful when none of the names was familiar.

After the war, Conroy's home state published a three-volume accounting of every resident of Connecticut who had served in the military and the medical corps. The books contain endless pages of names, 20 or so to a page, arranged by hometown and annotated with basic biographical data—place of birth, age at enlistment, details of service, etc. Stars are sprinkled throughout the volumes to mark the service members who died. Sometimes there are no stars displayed on a two-page spread. These are the good pages because that means everyone who went into the service came out alive.

Those entries marked with stars bear a grim code to signify how someone died. KIA, killed in action. DW, died of wounds. DD, died of disease. Occasionally the whiff of a story accompanies a listing. "Died of accidental drowning Aug 4/17," meaning August 4, 1917. "Died of suicide, gunshot wound, Jan 14/18." "Was on board the U.S.S. *Leimster* when the vessel was torpedoed and sunk Oct 10/18." Some service members died in action maddeningly close to the end of combat.

Illnesses such as tuberculosis, meningitis, influenza, and pneumonia claimed countless lives, as shown in the directories. Many men died in hospitals long after the war ended, perhaps from their wounds or from the residual effects of poisonous gas. Most entries for the deceased include a concluding fact or two, perhaps the location of someone's grave at an American military cemetery in France or an indication of who received notification of the death. Often a mother's name and address is given, or else a father's. Sometimes the person notified was a sister, an aunt, or simply just "a friend."

"The old company has changed a lot now," observed a sergeant from the 101st Infantry during the summer of 1918. "A lot of old faces are missing and new ones take their places and soon the original company will be only a fond memory of the past." He concluded, "They are going one by one."

Soldiers witnessed unspeakably horrid deaths: compatriots blown apart by artillery fire, drained of life force while bleeding to death, or strangled by the suffocating effects of poisonous gas. Conroy inevitably lost friends in battle, and he would have witnessed an almost daily dose of carnage during the summer campaigns. Stubby's survival, like that proverbial cat, as Conroy later wrote, must have given him comfort, and even hope, that the pair of them would come through the war alive, somehow.

Even in death, there was little dignity. Bodies lay exposed for hours—or days—before they could be buried. The summer sun magnified the smell of death as soldiers coped with the grisly triage of combat: first tend the living, then the dead. Enemy fire just added to the challenges, as did the disposal of the enormous corpses of horses killed in combat. "Well, ma," one soldier wrote home, "if we kick off we are surely going to heaven because we are now doing our hitch in hell." Another, after fighting and then being tasked with burying the dead, observed, "First we are soldiers, then undertakers."

Given such alternatives, becoming a prisoner of war might not have seemed so bad. That summer the Germans surrendered in droves. Some gave up willingly—even prematurely—such as the eight men who surrendered to a startled Army Signal Corps photographer after they mistook his tripod and hand-cranking film camera for some sort of weapon. Raised arms and a call of "Kamerad" served as the standard signal of German surrender, but such appeals aroused suspicion at best (after doughboys learned the hard way that such appeals were sometimes tricks) and vengeance at worst. German machine-gunners, in particular, were lucky to ever be taken alive.

The fast-moving Allies literally scooped up prisoners of war by the hundreds. Although Conroy had not learned German, as a member of the intelligence unit of his company he no doubt helped to question the captured soldiers as a way to gain additional information about their troop movements. Stubby aided the processing of new prisoners of war by helping to keep them in orderly formations as they marched through camp, and "woe to the German who would step a foot out of line." He acquired such a dislike of Germans—identifying them, reportedly, through a combination of smell and the recognition of their foreign uniforms and speech—that eventually "it was found necessary to tie him up when batches of prisoners were being brought back [from the front], for fear that trouserless Germans would reach the prison pens."

Replacement troops—many of them newly arrived and undertrained—stepped up to fill the vacancies created within the ranks of the YD and other American outfits. The new soldiers hailed from all regions of the United States, and they added their own accents and backgrounds to the corps. The division's nickname may have seemed like an odd fit for service members born and bred south of the Mason-Dixon Line, but these men bonded with their Yankee brothers over a shared patriotic spirit. A Louisiana-born physician in the division observed, "If a German gets out alive, it won't be the fault of these boys."

For the rest of July, the Yankee Division pressed on with other Allied forces, turning each upcoming wheat field, patch of woodland, or occasional village into the next objective. By the time the fighting ended, with a general routing of the Germans from their recent territorial gains, Stubby, Conroy, and the soldiers of the 26th had advanced through 11 miles of hostile territory. They were parted from more than 750 comrades in the assault, and almost 4,200 received wounds. Overall, the Americans lost nearly 50,000 men in the second battle of the Marne. The campaign had been costly, but it confirmed that Germany was losing its gamble in the race against the mobilization of U.S. troops. Transport ships kept disgorging thousands of fresh

U.S. Army engineers used boats and boards to construct their first pontoon bridge across the Marne during the summer offensive against the Germans, east of Paris. This temporary span, which went into use on July 20, 1918, replaced the damaged structure shown in the background of the photo.

American doughboys on the shores of France, and the German army was on the defensive.

Stubby earned an unexpected reward following the conclusion of the summer fighting: a uniform. His handmade jacket came courtesy of the female residents of Château-Thierry, one of the cities liberated in the recent campaign, as a thank you for his skill and hard work. According to a story passed down by Conroy through his family, Stubby earned the garment because he had detected an impending gas bombardment of the town.

By sounding his doggy alarm, he had protected not just his fellow doughboys but the citizens of Château-Thierry, too. Such a feat would help explain why the jacket came into being.

Whether a few women or as many as a hundred of them contributed to the garment's creation is another matter of debate. It seems likely that the coat itself was fashioned by one or at most a few women only, but scores could well have had a hand in its decoration. The tan chamois-leather garment was sized to snap shut under the dog's belly and button under his neck. Braided cord spelled out his name and military outfit on one side, and official U.S. military patches over the dog's shoulders attested to his service in the Yankee Division.

The jacket's pièce de résistance was an embroidered emblem that decorated the center of the garment. This piece of silk thread-work could easily have been passed among many women, as can be the custom for stitchery that is worn into battle (the idea being that multiple hands imbue a sort of collective protection to the wearer of the creation). The resulting design, later appliquéd to the jacket, depicted a wreath of colorful flags, one for each of the Allied nations.

Apparently no French woman rushed to make clothes for Fanny, a newer mascot in the 102nd Infantry, but her owner did. Edward Simpson, a cook for Company K, had purchased the goat while stationed in the Toul sector. Fanny, aka "the Kaiser's goat," had kept pace with the kitchen during the advancing summer campaign. Her diet was, naturally, voracious and varied. She reportedly ate everything from cigarette butts to chocolate cookies.

As the war progressed, other mascots materialized, too. There was Rags, a shaggy mutt discovered by an American soldier on the streets of Paris after first being mistaken for his fabric namesake; his rescuer brought him back to the First Division and put him to work delivering messages. There was Belle, the setter, who was separated from her Marine owner until they coincidentally ended up at the same field hospital. And among other examples, there was Philly, who shared Stubby's story of having been smuggled as a stray to France; she served as mascot for the U.S. 315th Infantry Regiment that originated, naturally, in Philadelphia.

In August, with fighting winding down around the Marne, the weary Yankee Division doughboys left the war zone behind at last. There were no trick trains this time, and, for Conroy and Stubby anyway, Paris became a satisfying place to visit instead of just a mirage on a distant skyline. The pair shared ten days there during Conroy's furlough from combat duty.

The one story that survives from this visit takes on the feel of a tall tale. "On duty or on vacation Stubby was always ready to perform some act of kindness or deed of heroism," explained a *Washington Post* reporter in a 1925 summary of the mascot's life. The newspaper recounts how Conroy and his small uniformed companion caught the attention of a pair of sisters in Paris near the Arc de Triomphe. The girls, who had been intent on crossing the street until they saw Stubby, stopped on the sidewalk to pet him. The dog loved the attention and nudged the younger sibling for further petting, causing the girls to delay their departure even longer. The story continued: "Not more than a minute had passed after the child approached Stubby when a runaway cab horse plunged madly up the street, directly in the path of what, but for Stubby, would have been the route chosen by his petite friend."

No one gave the dog a medal, but he gained yet another set of fans. The Yankee Division was helping to retake the lost territory of France, and Stubby, along for the adventure, was winning the hearts of soldier and civilian alike all along the way.

FRESNES-EN-WOEVRE, IN THE ST MIHIEL

PART TWO

WAR AND PEACE

WHERE TERRIFIC FIGHTING TOOK PLACE.

*Fresnes-en-Woëvre, one of the communities caught up in
the St. Mihiel campaign of September 1918, became a city
in name only as a result of combat during the Great War.*

August 6, 1918

★ ★ ★ ★ ★

The women appear single file, dressed all in white. Colors frame the steamy summer scene. The green leaves of overhanging trees. The red, white, and blue of the American flag borne by the first marcher. The purple, white, and gold banners of the figures who follow. These women, too, are off to do battle, off to do battle with the President of the United States. And all of Congress, if necessary.

Off to do battle armed with courage and cloth.

And words.

"How long must women wait for liberty?"

Letters stitched on fabric portray the battle cry. Panel after panel, hoisted aloft by silent sentinels, pass in review.

Onward the women march, 100 strong, until they reach their battlefield, the public space of Lafayette Square. An elevated base for the park's namesake statue becomes the high ground for their attack. The women's adversary lies in sight, across Pennsylvania Avenue, at home in the White House.

Ready, aim, fire.

A few words of demand. The vote, we want to vote. Maybe a dozen words spoken, but then they stop. One soldier down as a police officer hauls her from her stony platform.

Arrested.

The next soldier fires. She, too, is fighting for her right to vote. Not even a sentence lands, and then she is gone. Arrest silences her voice, too.

And the next. And the next.

Three, four, ten, forty-one, -two, -three. All are pulled aside and thrust into police wagons. Forty-five, -six, -seven. Silenced even as their banners flutter outside the windows of their captors' vans.

And then number forty-eight, the leader, just standing there, observing the scene, falls in the battle. Alice Paul. Arrested.

Fight over, supporters grow silent as their comrades head to court. And then to jail. And hunger strikes. Again. Fight over, but not abandoned.

The women will do battle another day. They, too, will fight until victory is won. Until women can vote equally with men.

President Wilson had said: "The world must be made safe for democracy."

All well and good for the world. But what about at home? What about democracy here?

★ CHAPTER SIX ★

THE HOME FRONT

WITH THE POSSIBLE EXCEPTIONS OF FURLOUGHS, booze, and loyal dogs, nothing served as a better antidote to weariness with war than thoughts of home. Soldiers clung to cherished photos. They mailed home letters filled with war-inspired revelations: "I appreciate luxuries, food, and home," an artilleryman wrote his family from the front. "I've learned what Liberty is, and to appreciate it," he acknowledged. They penned heartfelt doggerel for loved ones, such as these lines composed by a young recruit from Middleton, Connecticut:

> *And while gazing at the barb-wire for a sulking Boche*
> *or two,*
> *The thought of home and mother once again comes*
> *back to you.*
> *You can see her dear, sweet, smiling face while at your*
> *post you stand.*
> *She seems to give you grit to save that grimy blood-*
> *stained land.*

As with too many other correspondents, both the affectionate son and the artilleryman later died in combat.

Any letters exchanged between Robert Conroy and his family are lost to history, although the siblings must have corresponded given their close-knit relationships. Everything Conroy wrote would have been reviewed by military censors, and he would have known not to comment on his missions or his location. Stubby would have made an easy topic to share, and the family back in New Britain, Connecticut, probably gained an increasing sense of the dog's importance to the man. With Stubby at his side, Conroy must have seemed ready to handle whatever the conflict threw at them.

His siblings, meanwhile, were contributing to the war effort in their own ways. Conroy's oldest sister, Margaret, had married soon after the European battles began. She and her husband, Frank, shared a home with Margaret's three younger sisters. The extended family had vacated their childhood dwelling and moved to a more modest house across town on Church Street. Margaret's husband commuted to work in nearby Hartford while she stayed home with their young daughter and, before long, a baby boy.

Margaret's sister Alice, who had become blind due to a child-hood illness, stayed home with her, while their younger siblings took wartime jobs. Helen worked in the bookkeeping department of a local manufacturing company that was famous for invent-ing the first stovetop coffee percolator, among other household innovations. During the war her employer manufactured prod-ucts that supported the military cause. About this time Helen's twin, Gertrude, became a secretary for the local Red Cross office. Conroy's younger brother, Hugh, had enlisted in the military, too; he served stateside with the U.S. Army medical department, the sector that evaluated and cared for soldiers before or after their combat service, as well as overseas.

The extended-family household on Church Street may well have been one of the more than 13 million that displayed a pledge card as participants in the voluntary rationing of key household resources during the war. The U.S. government instituted the program in an effort to divert American goods to the battlefront. The conserved food was also used to combat hunger among the war-ravaged citizens of European Allies.

The government launched an extensive public relations campaign to encourage compliance with its goals. The publicity effort pitched the rationing program as a way to "Help your boy at the front." Posters appeared that proclaimed "Food will win the war." The government encouraged families to reduce their consumption of beef, pork, wheat, sugar, and fat. "Save the wheat for the fighters," proclaimed one sign. "Eat more cornmeal, rye flour, oatmeal, and barley."

The campaign relied on fostering a climate of habitual self-denial through peer pressure and appeals to patriotism. Thus families were urged to honor "meatless Mondays" and "wheatless Wednesdays." There were porkless days and calls to conserve on other staples. At its peak in early 1918, the suggested restrictions mushroomed into a dizzying schedule of demands: "Hereafter Mondays and Wednesdays will be observed as 'wheatless days,' and there will also be one wheatless meal each day. There will be one meatless day (Tuesday) and one meatless meal each day, and in addition, two porkless days (Tuesdays and Saturdays)."

Herbert Hoover, a future U.S. President, was tapped to head the program for President Wilson. Hoover exhorted Americans to stop eating whole wheat bread and switch to "victory bread," a baked good whose preparation evolved over a period of weeks until its wheat flour had been diluted to no more than 80 percent of the grain content. Women's organizations staged patriotic

U.S. flags hung patriotically over a firearms factory floor in Hartford, Connecticut, while women inspected parts for Colt .45 semiautomatic pistols, bound for the battlefields of France.

demonstrations for how to cook within the suggested rationing guidelines, and an army of volunteers, mostly housewives, distributed pledge cards across the nation to encourage compliance. A relentless publicity campaign assured that the goals of conservation seldom strayed far from the public's mind: "Eat less, and let us be thankful that we have enough to share with those who fight for freedom," advised one campaign poster.

Hoover's program wasn't the only one that sought to influence Americans through appeals to patriotism. With President Wilson's blessing, the federal government opened a propaganda office, known as the Committee on Public Information, or CPI, to generate public support for the war. This office, run by a former investigative reporter turned political operative named George Creel, produced promotional films about the war effort, created "war study" materials for public schools and universities, and crafted patriotic speeches that 75,000 volunteers delivered around the country as his army of so-called four-minute men (in a nod to the Revolutionary War heroes). One of the committee's chief responsibilities was to foster a sense of public obligation to buy war bonds. These choices, too, were cast as the home-front way to help the soldiers assure "that liberty shall not perish from the earth."

Thus, as is often the case during a war, patriotism and politics became interwoven on the home front in ways that were both commendable and concerning. Yes, compliance with the rationing helped the troops, and so did the purchasing of victory bonds. But what were citizens to make of the people who chose not to participate in these efforts? Should they be condemned or tolerated? What should be the limits of peer pressure during wartime?

The CPI campaign added to the tension by creating a negative backlash against the nation's visible German-American population. Posters portrayed the war effort as a battle against an evil Kaiser (who was often personified in artwork as the devil) and a brutal army of barbarians, the so-called Huns (who were depicted as lurking, blood-smeared hulks). By extension, everything pro-American was good; everything German became bad.

Anyone, American or otherwise, who questioned the war effort—from politicians to pastors—could be targeted for criticism, or worse. In some cases, people were tarred and feathered, or even lynched. German-American immigrants and their descendants gained particular scrutiny in such a climate, and anti-German hate crimes soared. Citizens burned German-language books, communities banned the teaching of German (in fact, foreign-language education, German and otherwise, would never recover its former popularity or vigor in the country), and squads of self-appointed vigilantes scoured their towns for traitors. Restaurants scrubbed their menus of sauerkraut and hamburgers, replacing them with liberty cabbage and liberty steak. Bars stopped serving pretzels. German measles turned into liberty measles. The works of German composers were shunned. Towns, businesses, and families replaced their German-sounding names with true-blue American ones.

The U.S. courts became clogged with cases that tested whether citizens' First Amendment rights of free speech should have prevented them from being jailed when they spoke out against the war. Eugene Debs, a founding member of the Socialist Party of America and a four-time presidential candidate, landed in prison after delivering a fiery antiwar speech in June 1918. He languished there until pardoned by Wilson's successor, President Warren G. Harding, at the end of 1921. (His court challenge failed to win the support of the U.S. Supreme Court, but later on other comparable cases did, establishing the case law that eventually supported the broad scope of rights we've come to expect from the First Amendment.)

A subtext of battles raged across the home front in the wake of the war's screaming cover of patriotism. Prohibition finally won passage in Congress, in part because the legislation penalized the largely German-American brewing industry. The nation's open-door policy toward immigrants slammed shut in the aftermath of the war, and a wave of postwar deportations assured that outspoken government critics, such as labor and social activist Emma Goldman and other immigrant radicals, lost their influence on the nation's soil. Labor leaders, socialists, communists, immigrants—anyone not toeing the with-us-or-against-us patriotic line—found themselves at risk of being silenced.

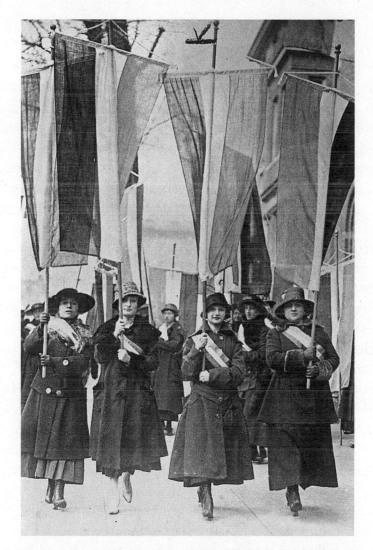

*Advocates for women's voting rights had already begun picketing
in front of the White House before the United States joined the
Great War; this photo captures factory workers as they hoist their
colors in solidarity on February 18, 1917. After Woodrow Wilson's
April call to arms, the women's continuing protests were
condemned as unpatriotic.*

Even woman suffragists, many of them members of the nation's middle- and upper-class society, became caught up in the political crosshairs of the times. By the beginning of the First World War, the fight for universal voting rights for women had already weathered a number of schisms and disagreements in its nearly 70-year history. Another split occurred during the 1910s and intensified after the United States joined the Allied war effort.

As a result, a new group of suffragists emerged under the leadership of a young firebrand named Alice Paul. Her organization, the National Woman's Party, appealed to a growing strain of militancy among frustrated activists. Early in 1917, these women became the first group in history to stage nonviolent protests in front of the White House. After the U.S. declaration of war, when other suffragists put down their banners to support the war effort, members of the National Women's Party persisted with their protests, even when its activists were labeled as unpatriotic, attacked by vigilante citizens, arrested, and imprisoned.

After the President pardoned jailed protesters in late 1917, the militant suffragists suspended their acts of civil disobedience, hopeful that their cause would at last advance. But legislation stalled once again, and they renewed their protests by picketing in Lafayette Square, across from the White House, starting on August 6, 1918. Although widely criticized at the time, their efforts during and after the war contributed to the ultimate ratification, in 1920, of the 19th Amendment, granting American women a universal right to vote.

Such political and social turmoil was probably not among the daily concerns in the Conroy household. There were children to tend, bills to pay, and jobs to do. Maybe the women at home shouldered extra war-time responsibilities, such as knitting socks for soldiers. Plus, of course, there were all those rationed meals to plan. Had the family eaten its wheatless meal of the day? Could corn oil really take the place of animal shortening? Was this a meatless day or just one that called for no pork?

Perhaps the elder Conroy sisters, while they worked around the house, voiced worries about their brother overseas, and surely they shared laughs over any Stubby stories that he sent home. Maybe their days, too, were brightened by the role this one dog was playing in their own family during what was otherwise a time of war.

★ CHAPTER SEVEN ★

FOLLIES AND FIREWORKS

WHEN ROBERT CONROY RETURNED FROM HIS AUGUST furlough, he—and presumably Stubby, too—saluted a new commander, Col. Hiram I. Bearss. "Machine Gun" Parker had been moved out of the 102nd Infantry during a shuffling of officers and been sent to command a regiment in a different division. Stubby apparently passed his salute test with "Hiking Hiram" (whose signature hiking accoutrement was the box of cigars he tucked under his arm), and by early September the mascot and Conroy were heading toward their next assignment.

The Yankee Division, fighting as part of an all-American force, was tasked with wresting from the Germans a 200-square-mile area south of Verdun that they had held since 1914. To affect the greatest chance of surprise, the U.S. troops mobilized under cover of darkness and on foot. Drizzling September rains, signaling the change of seasons, accompanied YD doughboys as they advanced toward their positions over the course of about ten days. Some of the men feasted on wild blackberries as they hiked ("My! But they tasted good."), but woe be to the soldier who splurged on cherries

("I never want to see a cherry again."). Even the camp cooks caught harvest fever, turning local apples into apple fritters, for example.

By September 12, 1918, when the attack began, Conroy and Stubby were part of a force of more than a half million U.S. soldiers, bolstered along the front by more than 100,000 French troops. The campaign in what was known as the St. Mihiel salient turned quickly into a rout. Within four days the Allies had swept the designated area of its German occupiers and liberated the city of St. Mihiel, although, truthfully, it helped that the Germans had already begun withdrawing from the region.

The campaign began with the usual nighttime barrage of artillery fire, accompanied by the seemingly ever present French rain. Soldiers advanced through daylight fog and continuing rain, moving so rapidly that once again they outpaced their rolling kitchens and lost their chance for a cooked supper. In some cases, artillery units, too, fell out of sync with the advancing infantrymen. In others, the Americans were able to overrun fortifications still immobilized by recent artillery fire. Conroy would have been kept busy as an observer during the drive, traversing the hilly terrain as he scouted the path of the German retreat.

When the French troops began to lag in their advances, General Pershing asked the Yankee Division to help close the resulting gap. Conroy's 102nd Regiment earned the assignment of marching into the night—having already advanced all day—in order to meet up with a partner force from the First Division at the French town of Vigneulles. The Germans had set so many storehouses and villages on fire during their retreat that the Americans could see a dozen or more blazes across the horizon as they raced toward their objective. The Yankees beat the Big Red One to Vigneulles, arriving at 2:30 in the morning, just in time to capture a retreating German supply train. The men worked hours more to secure the rest of the city.

Stubby, according to subsequent news reports, "was with the first troops to cross the front lines in the St. Mihiel drive, and was on hand to see the haul of prisoners made at Vigneulles and the surrounding towns." The pursuit of the Germans, which had begun on September 12, continued through the next day. Barbed wire was ever present, creating one more obstacle in the chase, but the capture of prisoners was surprisingly easy. Some were literally rousted from their beds. Many seemed delighted to be caught.

All that rain and mud had slowed down the Germans, too, and the Americans frequently overtook not just men but abandoned armaments and supplies. Soldiers turned up stores of personal luxuries, as well, from cigarettes and cigars to beer and cognac. "The Boche are a long ways from starved, by the looks of the kitchen," one Yankee Division man wrote home. The final haul was impressive: at least 100 artillery guns, hundreds of machine guns and trench mortar launchers, storehouses of ammunition, warehouses of supplies; all that, and 16,000 prisoners of war, too. The trade-off in losses was more favorable than usual: 7,000 American casualties overall, including 109 YD fatalities and fewer than 400 wounded.

General Pershing and his staff were ecstatic. The A.E.F.'s nightly field dispatch—an official snapshot of military highlights released to the news media and American public—swelled in length from its usual clipped sentence or two into full paragraphs of praise. The September 14 communiqué gushed: "The dash and vigor of our troops and of the Valiant French divisions which fought shoulder to shoulder with them is shown by the fact that the forces attacking on both faces of the salient effected a junction and secured the results desired within 27 hours." The residents of St. Mihiel offered an even better form of praise; they gave hugs and kisses to the liberating troops. Perhaps Stubby earned a particularly savory bone, or at least some grateful petting.

The American soldiers had little opportunity to savor their victory, however. Pershing had committed them for service in a larger Allied effort, the Meuse-Argonne campaign, a massive operation designed to secure Germany's unconditional surrender. Unfortunately this front was 60 miles away from St. Mihiel. Pershing had tapped a young colonel named George C. Marshall to coordinate the massive transfer of men and matériel from St. Mihiel and other sites to the final front.

Historian Edward G. Lengel details Marshall's execution of this colossal exercise in his commanding history of the Meuse-Argonne campaign, *To Conquer Hell*. Lengel observes: "It was the biggest logistical undertaking in the history of the U.S. Army, before or since. In two weeks, 600,000 men, 4,000 guns, 90,000 horses, and

French rains turned unpaved roads into mud-filled obstacle courses for U.S. military convoys when they headed toward the Meuse-Argonne front in the fall of 1918.

almost a million tons of supplies" had to traverse the gap between the fronts. Oh, and for added kicks, the transfer was supposed to happen secretly, if possible at night. The French climate contributed almost constant rain to the undertaking. Pershing gave Marshall the assignment fewer than three weeks before the offensive's eventual start date: September 26. Marshall met the challenge.

The Yankee Division drew an assignment due north of the recently liberated Vigneulles. Conroy and Stubby moved into position with their comrades, tasked with leading a pair of diversionary raids on two German-held towns east of Verdun, Marchéville and Riaville. These attacks, scheduled to coincide with the early morning start of the true offensive, were designed to confuse the Germans and force them to hold troops in this defensive area that might otherwise be rushed as reinforcements against the broader assault. It was a sound plan, but its execution met with as many obstacles as were encountered during the opening hours and days of the larger Meuse-Argonne campaign itself. Objectives that were supposed to be easy to reach proved deadly to attain, and the associated hopes for staying on schedule and gaining momentum through surprise proved elusive.

Stubby's historical record is full of contradicting "facts," and the circumstances surrounding one of his most lauded achievements are among the most muddled. The event clearly took place, and September 26 seems the most likely date for it to have occurred, the same day the 102nd set out to capture Marchéville. Thus it seems, even as the Americans continued to reel in German prisoners of war, Stubby managed to capture one all on his own. Whether the man was lost or conducting surveillance, whether he was hiding in shrubbery or discovered in the open, must be left to the reader's imagination. All scenarios have been suggested.

Whatever the setup, what came next seems beyond dispute. Stubby approached the hapless man and gave no credence to the usual German plea of "Kamerad." Any German doggy speech that the man may have mustered went unheeded as well. Out of ideas, the soldier turned and fled. This strategy, too, proved ineffective. Stubby bounded after him and showed himself to be by far the faster of the two. One story suggests that the dog chased his captive toward his friends on the American lines. Others counter that he lunged at the fleeing man and knocked him flat, the dog's jaws clamped on the seat of the soldier's pants (and presumably a healthy chunk of his flesh). Humans, already alerted by Stubby's barked alarms, arrived to complete the apprehension.

Details aside, the accomplishment earned the mascot more than praise and admiration. Some say it won the dog official rank in the U.S. military—hence his eventual nickname, Sergeant Stubby. However, there is no supporting documentation for such a claim, and his designation as a sergeant appears to be more a recent folk legend than an established fact from his lifetime. Without a doubt, though, the capture netted Stubby one of the war's most treasured icons of battlefront booty: a German Iron Cross. The dog's captive had received the award for previous military service. Informal rules of engagement awarded such spoils to the captor, and thus Stubby by rights deserved the decoration. Conroy dutifully added the medal to his friend's jacket, eventually positioning it playfully so that it hung disrespectfully beneath the dog's stub of a tail.

The ambitious Meuse-Argonne campaign, which had begun with lofty expectations in late September, devolved quickly into murky, bloody mayhem. Objectives that should have been reached in hours took weeks to achieve. Unreliable and primitive means of communication left commanders and soldiers alike out of touch and out of sync. Thousands of men were thrown needlessly into the paths of invincible machine-gun fire. Some replacement troops were so poorly trained that they had to ask, just prior to battle, how to attach their ammunition clips to their guns or what they needed to do to "fix" (as in, affix) what looked like an unbroken bayonet. These newcomers entered the fray unprepared in ways that elevated the risks for all the soldiers around them.

As the campaign dragged on, first for days and then for weeks, fighters lost track of when they'd last bathed or shaved. Soldiers became too tired to fight, too scared to fight, too discouraged to fight. Meals might or might not show up on schedule. Tens of thousands of men began straggling, falling behind as their units advanced, losing the motivation to keep up. Meanwhile, rain continued and the temperatures began to fall, giving the summer uniform–clad soldiers two more reasons to be miserable.

Did Conroy's spirits lag along with the other men? How many friends had he lost by this point in the war? Did he advance apprehensively through the forward ground he was tasked with surveying? Or had he settled into a mental zone where he lived each day as just another day, each moment still alive as the moment that mattered most? Maybe Conroy followed the example of his best friend, a being who, when he anticipated anything beyond the moment, simply looked forward to the creature comforts of food, sleep, and companionship. "The dog may have been what got him through the war," Conroy's grandson would later say. Maybe Stubby didn't just keep Conroy company while they hiked across France. Maybe he helped him see beyond the horror and uncertainty of combat to the beauty of just being alive. It would have helped.

During the fall of 1918, soldiers experienced terrifying scenes of combat and death during the Meuse-Argonne campaign. Witness two companies of the 312th Infantry Regiment, advancing toward an objective under the cover of fog, until they were caught in machine-gun crossfire because the fog lifted; those who survived the bullets had to feign death until nightfall before they could

113

safely retreat. Witness Brig. Gen. Douglas MacArthur, who led a reconnaissance mission where he alone survived an unexpected artillery barrage. Witness the artillery batteries that were singled out for sniping missions—firing on obscured German batteries in an effort to provoke return fire that would reveal their locations, and then scrambling to clear themselves and their equipment from the area before the arrival of the invited counter-shelling.

The so-called Lost Battalion experienced one of the more harrowing trials of the First World War. This outfit from the 77th Division fell out of communication with its flanking troops as they advanced into unfriendly territory. Before they realized it, they had outpaced their compatriots and been cut off on all sides by German forces. Maj. Charles Whittlesey, the battalion commander, attempted to signal his distress—delivered by carrier pigeons—but failed to adequately convey the peril of their situation. The men had advanced with only a day's rations, and the Germans kept them pinned in place, at first for one day and then for a second.

At one point, an American artillery barrage, presumably intended for the Germans, began falling on the trapped U.S. soldiers. Whittlesey entrusted his last remaining pigeon with a plea to stop the shelling. However, this bird, upon its release, flew not toward its homing station but into a tree. It took flight only after a daring doughboy climbed up after it and startled it aloft. The bird, known as Cher Ami, became famous for delivering the message. Coincidentally or not, the shelling stopped. But not until the fourth day of the battalion's isolation did American troops dislodge the Germans sufficiently to secure its relief. By that point, 216 of the battalion's 554 members had died and another 144 were too fatigued or wounded to walk from the scene.

Comparatively speaking, the Yankee Division was faring much better. Two weeks into the Meuse-Argonne campaign, as October unfolded and other soldiers continued to fight, the YD men

*The 26th Division captured more than 3,000 German soldiers
during the First World War, including these men
on November 10, 1918, one day before the cease-fire.*

earned a brief reprieve from warfront service. Having completed its late-September diversionary raids, the troops began to move toward the main front. Along the way they passed through Verdun for a break. Stubby "played around here for a week just before entering the Meuse-Argonne drive," reported Conroy, and the dog's antics entertained the soldiers while they regrouped.

At about the same time, General Pershing turned over command of the bulk of the American fighting forces to Lt. Gen. Hunter Liggett. This mid-October change freed the A.E.F. commander to focus on broader administrative and diplomatic duties, including the anticipated negotiation of Germany's surrender. That Germany would surrender had become certain. Only the timing of when it would do so remained in doubt.

Because the fall campaign had failed to progress as planned, Liggett insisted that his men had to pause and regroup. He recommended that the Allies renew their coordinated assault at the end of the month. During the intervening two weeks, some troops would keep up the fight while others rested and shifted positions. Two types of military actions took place during the "lull." Some were designed to secure more advantageous starting ground for the renewed offensive; others, including ones manned by the Yankee Division, were meant to distract the Germans at their flanks, thus preventing them from reinforcing the midsection of the line where the Allies planned to focus its final assault.

The Germans maintained a nearly impenetrable series of fortifications all along the Meuse-Argonne front, the so-called Hindenburg Line. They had held the territory since 1914 and had constructed a sequence of three trenches in its defense; the Allies knew its conquest would be difficult and costly. These defensive lines had been carved into a territory that stretched to a depth of 12 miles behind No Man's Land. Each of the bands of trenches bore the name of a witch from one of Richard Wagner's operas, with the middle one—the *Kriemhilde Stellung*—serving as the strongest line of defense. Allied forces had penetrated the fortifications in places during the opening days of the Meuse-Argonne campaign in late September, but overall the line still held.

One of Pershing's last orders, before he relinquished his operational command to General Liggett, hit the Yankee Division with the force of an incoming artillery barrage: Pershing relieved General Edwards of his command. On October 22, the YD leader learned that he was being ordered back to the States to help with further training there. Fodder for the transfer had been accumulating throughout the war. The two career Army officers had conflicting styles, backgrounds, and temperaments. Even more significantly, Pershing had a bias against National Guard troops, favoring such regular Army units as the Big Red One over the Yankee Division. He had even referred to the Yankee men as Boy Scouts, a dig at the presumed inferior training and fortitude of citizen soldiers originating in the National Guard versus the professional fighters of the nation's small standing Army. Accomplishments notwithstanding, Pershing tended to focus on the faults of the division under Edwards's command rather than celebrating what had gone right. Pershing tapped Brig. Gen. Frank Bamford to take Edwards's place.

The loss of their beloved "Daddy" stunned the Yankee Division soldiers. Morale plummeted. Straggling, which had never before been high with this division, began to rise. Conroy's spirits surely must have dropped. Even Stubby, who had befriended the general, would have missed the congenial leader. Edwards had had a way of motivating the men to accept every assignment as a new challenge that could be tackled with Yankee grit and ingenuity. After his departure, that fighting spirit would be tested without the benefit of his leadership by some of the division's worst combat yet.

On October 16, just a few days before Edwards was relieved of his command, his soldiers had returned to duty, this time on the right flank of the Allied lines, north of Verdun. Initially the men were tasked with wresting advantageous high ground from the Germans. Doing so proved difficult and deadly. Then, just as Edwards relinquished his command, his men were thrown into a series of almost endlessly fruitless assaults against the Hindenburg Line, all designed to keep the Germans focused on their flank so that they could not shift troops elsewhere along the defenses. U.S. casualties ran high, and the men became exhausted as their ranks thinned, even as orders kept coming to advance. Add the ever present mud and rain plus the hardship of transporting food to the embattled troops, and it's not surprising that morale continued to fall.

On November 1, the overall Meuse-Argonne assault resumed. Once again the Allies threw their full force against the Hindenburg Line, but this time they were better positioned and more effective in their assaults. Artillery barrages and gas shells softened up the German front lines, and long-held defenses began to give way. In some places the Allies burst past the first line with such force that their opponents abandoned not only it but the *Kriemhilde Stellung*, their more heavily fortified middle trench, too. Instead of advancing by the yard, the Allies advanced by the mile. Even when the Germans gave ground reluctantly, the Americans fought fiercely and relentlessly.

While the overall campaign continued, the Yankee Division persisted with its slower, diversionary work in what was dubbed the Neptune sector of the front, so named because of its location at the outermost orbit of the battle territory (during an era when Neptune represented the most distant orbiting body in the solar system; Pluto had yet to be discovered). Casualties mounted as ground was taken and lost and taken again. Even with reinforcements, the infantry regiments remained under strength, and all up and down the lines the soldiers were wet, hungry, demoralized, and in need of rest.

The Americans, who lagged behind the Germans in their use of poison gas, increased their employment of it late in the war. Meanwhile the Germans continued to routinely bombard Allied forces with gas-filled shells. All of the chemical agents they used distressed the lungs; mustard gas, the latest German innovation, caused painful blistering and, often, at least temporary blindness, too. Soldiers coated their bodies with a greasy paste nicknamed sag in an effort to protect their skin, and they continued to wear gas masks when called for, but such precautions were not foolproof. Plus, sometimes gas arrived so unexpectedly that advance preparation was impossible.

No one recorded what type of gas overcame Robert Conroy on November 2, or under what circumstances, but his exposure was serious enough to require hospitalization. Some accounts suggest that Stubby, too, was injured in the attack and that he and Conroy recuperated together at a field hospital. This injury served as Conroy's only battlefield casualty and is listed in his military records as "wounded in action, slightly."

Once again the mascot's presence proved fortuitous. He reportedly attracted the interest of a Red Cross nurse during one of his prowls around the facility; she followed him out of curiosity, and, when they reached Conroy's bunk, she recognized the wounded soldier as an acquaintance from New Britain. "Stubby was a messenger of friendship," noted the reporter who retold the tale. Perhaps thanks to the added care of Nurse Borg, Conroy recovered quickly. He and his ever present friend were back at the front as the war came to a close.

By November 10, commanders understood that the fighting was scheduled to stop the next day, 11/11, at 11 a.m. Nonetheless, they continued to order Allied assaults, motivated, perhaps, by a mixture of habit, ambition, and the belief that they needed to remind the Germans of the Allied determination to keep fighting. The final two days of Yankee Division combat proved just as fruitless and just as deadly as the ones that had preceded them. Straggling peaked among soldiers determined not to die after having survived all the previous months of warfare. In contrast, many artillery batteries approached that final morning of combat as a team challenge. Could they launch all of their remaining shells before being ordered to cease fire? Some batteries ignored the temptation, but others took it up, often triggering a reciprocal response from the opposing side.

One A.E.F. soldier recorded the minute-by-minute scene at a nearby gunnery. At 10:59, one minute before cease-fire, he noted,

An Army Signal Corps photographer documented this battery from the Seventh Field Artillery during operations in the St. Mihiel salient, September 1918. Later that month, Capt. Harry S. Truman told the gunners in his battery from the 129th Field Artillery that "I'd rather be right here than be President of the United States." After his crew discharged some 3,000 shells during the opening hours of the Meuse-Argonne campaign, the future President reported being "deaf as a post."

"The guns are so hot that the paint is rising from them in blisters. The crews are sweating despite the autumn chill of the air. To them the peace approaches as a regrettable interruption." When 11 a.m. arrived, he wrote: "The silence is oppressive. It weighs in on one's eardrums."

Such a silence fell all along the line, signaling safety for troops pinned down under fire. Suddenly natural sounds, even the dripping of moisture from branches, were audible once more. Some soldiers began to cheer; others just went off in search of hot food.

Conroy and "hundreds of friends crowded around Stubby," when the cease-fire arrived. "Many credited him with causing the gods to yield the good luck of victory."

Military dispatch writers searched for the right words for sharing the news. Every evening since May 15, 1918, the U.S. command post had been issuing a report of battlefront highlights. For a few weeks, as the war drew to a close, two reports were issued daily. These messages offered a snapshot of warfront events to the media and general public. Some of the communiqués conveyed moments of calm: "June 22 (No. 39).—The day passed quietly at all positions held by our troops" and "July 13 (No. 60).—There is nothing of importance to report." Others offered clipped summaries of horrific days of fighting: "July 17 (No. 64).—N.W. of Château-Thierry the enemy yesterday repeated his attempt of the preceding day to penetrate our lines near Vaux. His attack was completely broken up by our infantry and artillery fire before reaching our lines."

Now, thanks to the armistice, the military command would have no cause to write, as they had on August 2, "Last night our aviators successfully bombed the railroad station and yards at Conflans," or, as released the next day, "The full fruits of victory in the counter-offensive begun so gloriously by Franco-American troops on July 18 were reaped today when the enemy, who met his second great defeat on the Marne, was driven in confusion beyond the line of the Vesle . . ."

The dispatch for November 11 avoided hyperbole and boasting. Maybe the writers were exhausted, just like everyone else, or perhaps they knew that, in this case, less was more. So, with its more typical, dry brevity, the communiqué stated: "November 11, morning (No. 197).—In accordance with the terms of the armistice, hostilities on the fronts of the American Armies were suspended at 11 o'clock this morning."

The troops on the ground felt no compunction to keep their emotions in check. As the reality set in, the celebrations began. Bonfires sprang up all along the battle lines. Soldiers luxuriated in the heat and the possibility of drying out their clothes. Despite orders forbidding it, some Americans crossed into No Man's Land and fraternized with their former adversaries. There was jubilation among the Germans, too. Anyone who had survived such a war, whether victorious or not, could celebrate being alive. During some encounters, the Americans traded their extra cigarettes for German military souvenirs. At others, they collaborated on finding and burying their dead.

Conroy left no record of how he and Stubby celebrated in the hours that followed the cease-fire. Perhaps he still had work to do for the regimental commander. Maybe Stubby helped the medics locate the last of the wounded men. Or maybe they, too, had the freedom to savor the moments of silence, add their voice and bark to the cheers of relief, and settle into a warm spot for a mutual exchange of companionship and affection. Stubby, of course, wouldn't have understood the men who told him, "We're going home!" But he certainly would have shared their excitement.

That night the Germans took a cue from the morning's artillery gunners. This time, though, they raided their supplies of signal flares. These colored tracers had communicated military commands during the chaos of battle. The month before, a resourceful U.S. lieutenant had even co-opted this code for his own advantage during combat. His company, hesitant and exhausted, lacked the motivation to advance toward its next objective. The lieutenant coaxed his men into a favorable position and then, after nightfall, without them realizing that he had done so, he shot off a captured German signal flare. His men, who assumed the Germans had fired the flare, knew the green sparks meant one thing: incoming artillery. At the lieutenant's urging, the horrified soldiers rushed toward the relative safety of their objective, fleeing the shelter they had previously been reluctant to depart.

On the evening of the armistice, though, the colors of the signal flares lost their meanings of attack and warning and distress. All up and down the old Hindenburg Line, showers of sparks arced across the sky. Plenty of questions remained: When would the troops head home? To what surrender terms would the Germans be held? Would the Americans have to stay on to enforce the cease-fire?

Such worries dissolved in the enchantment of colored sparks. For once, no one was under fire, and both sides could savor the improvised repurposing of weaponry into a celebration of peace.

★ CHAPTER EIGHT ★

ARMISTICE

"THE BLOODIEST BATTLE IN AMERICAN HISTORY" IS HOW historian Edward G. Lengel characterizes the Meuse-Argonne campaign. It lasted 47 days from its start on September 26 to the armistice on November 11, 1918. According to Lengel, almost half of the casualties suffered by U.S. troops during the First World War were concentrated into these closing seven weeks of battle. More than 95,000 men were wounded during this span, and more than 26,000 died in action or from combat wounds.

Lengel states, "No single battle in American military history, before or since, even approaches the Meuse-Argonne in size and cost, and it was without question the country's most critical military contribution to the Allied cause in the First World War. And yet, within a few years of its end, nobody seemed to realize that it had taken place."

The idea that this battle—and, indeed, the war as a whole, really—would be largely forgotten some day was unfathomable in 1918. Army dispatch by Army dispatch, mile by mile, French town by French town, folks back home had followed the war's movement and could recite its progression from battlefront to battlefront almost with the confidence of a veteran. Meanwhile the soldiers, many of whom may have wanted to forget at least some aspects of the war, would bear its marks, inside if not out, for the rest of their lives.

Sgt. John J. Curtin, the Yankee Division soldier Stubby had aroused to safety during a gas attack in the spring of 1918, was among the survivors at war's end. By November, his tribute to Stubby could chronicle the dog's good fortune, too:

> *North of Verdun were our hardest battles,*
> *And many brave men gave death rattles,*
> *But Stubby came through hell O.K.*
> *And is ready to go back to the U.S.A.*

Some semblance of the YD had made it through the war, as well. The division had entered the conflict at full strength with 28,000 men, but the summer campaigns, the closing battles from the Meuse-Argonne campaign, and even the spreading influenza epidemic had all helped to thin its ranks tremendously. Despite the periodic arrival of reinforcements, the division's outfits never managed to close the gaps created by continual attrition.

At war's end, for example, one of the division's four infantry regiments could muster only 240 fighters when it should have had 3,000. Not all of the absent men were dead. True, 2,281 had been killed in action or died because of combat injuries, but more than 11,000 had been wounded and yet survived. Perhaps a third of these men had been wounded severely enough to leave the battle-field permanently maimed or disabled.

Such costs had not been paid without rewards. Yankee Division historian Michael E. Shay points out that the division ranked eighth out of the war's 29 most-active U.S. divisions in total territory gained under fire; when added up, its wartime advances totaled 28 miles. Additionally, the YD had captured more than 3,000 prisoners of war, including the one Stubby had seized. Only one division, the Big Red One, had served more days on the front line: 220 versus the Yankees' 193. Considering that such figures exclude travel time to and from points of service and that only 284 days had elapsed between the first of February, the month when the Yankee Division entered into combat service, and Armistice Day on November 11, it becomes clear that the men truly had gone to Europe to fight.

When Brig. Gen. Frank Bamford, the division's new commander, was asked on November 11 if his men could serve as part of the occupation army in Germany, he indicated that, as one reporter put it, "the division was in no condition to go on." Frank P. Sibley, that embedded correspondent from the *Boston Globe*, described the postwar soldiers thusly: "They were unshaven, red-eyed from days and days without sleep, hoarse so that some could not speak above a whisper. They were unbelievably caked in mud. They stank." Six hundred at a time, the men took turns traveling to Verdun for 12-hour leaves. There they were "rested up, fed, bathed, given fresh clothing from top to toe," and returned "clean and shaved," and much restored.

On November 14, the Sixth Division arrived to relieve the YD of its latest role on the front, peacekeeping. The men of the 26th bid the trenches farewell and headed away from the front lines toward reserve camps. There they and other soldiers would remain at the ready as a reminder of the forces at hand should treaty negotiations lag and the cease-fire not hold. If all went according to plan, though, doughboys would start queuing up to return home.

The Yankee Division's journey would be a slow one, and, for most of the men, it began literally one step at a time. Shouldering

*Tremendous relief, as well as considerable jubilation, followed
the cease-fire of the Great War on November 11, 1918.
Post-Armistice, this Belgian work dog made the rounds
pulling a cart loaded with bottles of beer.*

their 60-pound packs, the soldiers hiked more than 100 miles
from the war zone toward their next home, the community of
Montigny-le-Roi. Their route through the French countryside
traced the upstream course of the Meuse River, a tributary of
the Seine that had been an almost ever present landmark during
their service. They walked south, past Verdun, past St. Mihiel,
past lands that adjoined the Toul region and Seicheprey, where
Stubby had been wounded months before.

For something like eight days they trekked onward, even traveling through Neufchâteau, site of their previous winter's camp,
before reaching their intended destination. This time the rolling
kitchens kept up, and the weather gave the travelers a break—
cold, but little rain. Every footfall put each man one step closer to
home. More than likely, Robert Conroy and Stubby hiked right

along with everyone else. Artillery units and other special forces proceeded at a different pace. Battery crews, for example, had to deliver their guns to railroad stations and turn in their weary draft animals.

General Bamford's leadership of the Yankee Division lasted not even a month. Maj. Gen. Harry C. Hale, a friend and West Point classmate of General Edwards, took over his old friend's command on November 18. The troops had never warmed to Bamford; Hale they served more willingly, although he never eclipsed the standing in their minds of "Daddy" Edwards.

As they settled into billets in the area around Montigny-le-Roi, the doughboys of the 26th Division began to encounter something they hadn't seen in ages: bed sheets. In recent months the men had camped in tents, settled into ditches, made improvised bunks out of hay and evergreen branches, slept in mud puddles, and even occupied old German dugouts, encountering not only the familiar body lice but previously unseen red biting fleas. Their camping days over, Stubby and Conroy shared space with others from their regimental headquarters company, sleeping indoors for what could have been the first time in weeks.

These new and improved postwar quarters began filling up with familiar faces, including wounded service members who had been reassigned after their recoveries to random outfits for the duration of the war. Now these men were allowed to return to their original units, the ones that had most felt like home. Prisoners of war materialized, too. Many of these soldiers had missed almost all of the division's service, having been captured early on during the April raids at Seicheprey. These men had lived out the war in their own version of hell, particularly early on when the Germans felt certain of victory. After the war's tide turned in July, their conditions began to improve; perhaps, as one soldier suggested, their captors "realized that they would have to account for all they did." Even so, plenty of former prisoners required hospital care before they could rejoin their units.

On Christmas Day, President Woodrow Wilson himself paid the division a visit. Not only did he meet many of the men during his daylong stay; he met the division's number one mascot, too. Details of the encounter went unrecorded, but Stubby and Conroy would have crossed paths with the President at least once during the day's series of events. First off, representatives from the 102nd Infantry Regiment were on hand to greet the chief executive when he and his wife arrived at the train station of the nearby city of Chaumont.

Next, General Pershing and other dignitaries accompanied the presidential party by car to a field north of Langres so that he could review representatives of the troops, including members of the 102nd Infantry. Although the winter of 1919 was generally milder than the previous year's had been, its Christmas Day proved to be notably cold and dreary for northern France. Nonetheless, thousands of locals and soldiers were on hand to greet Wilson at the improvised parade ground.

The review of the troops took place on a sodden field in front of a modest, temporary viewing stand that sported patriotic bunting. General Pershing opened the event with words of greeting, and then the President, who was known for his oratorical skills, made a brief speech. He concluded his laudatory remarks by saying:

I feel a comradeship with you today which is delightful. As I look down upon these undisturbed fields and think of the terrible scenes through which you have gone, and realize how the quiet of peace, the tranquility of settled hopes, has descended upon us, while it is hard to be far from home, I can bid you a Merry Christmas, and I can, I think, confidently promise you a Happy New Year, and I can from the bottom of my heart say, God bless you.

The field Wilson surveyed may have been undisturbed by war, but it had taken its share of punishment from the weather. As various military bands played appropriate marching music, the assembled troops slogged through well-churned mud to parade past the reviewing stand. A small press corps documented the event on still and moving film.

Another crowd of citizens and soldiers greeted the President in Montigny-le-Roi, along with the band of the 102nd Regiment. The musicians played the American national anthem as the President and Mrs. Wilson prepared to join a group of officers for their midday Christmas meal. (Earlier plans to include rank-and-file doughboys had given way to a party for the higher-ups instead.) Guests feasted on traditional fare, including roasted chicken, roasted turkey and dressing, mashed potatoes and other vegetables, bread and butter, cranberry sauce, and pumpkin pies with coffee.

Army staffers had created an elaborate souvenir program booklet, bound by a red, blue, and white–spangled ribbon, to commemorate the occasion. Its color-illustrated pages not only displayed the day's menu, they also outlined the history of the division's military service. The art on the back cover conveyed the New Year's hope of all the troops: It pictured an ocean liner steaming across the Atlantic toward the western setting sun. After the meal, as his entourage made its way back to the train station, Wilson stopped to inspect several billets of members of the 102nd Regiment. Somewhere in the course of all these events and travels, the President not only met Stubby but, according to several reports, shook his paw.

While the Americans waited for their New Year's homecoming wish to come true, their dress uniforms began to hang heavy with medals. Some soldiers had distinguished themselves in battle and received commendations from the French military, even the signature Croix de Guerre decoration. But all combat veterans who had helped to liberate specific cities qualified for the various municipal medals awarded by grateful residents. Verdun. Château-Thierry. St. Mihiel. Conroy and fellow YD doughboys qualified for them all. Conroy and others also earned commemorative medals from the nation of France and from Marshal Foch, commander of French forces.

Medals hung from white ribbons and from red ribbons trimmed with blue and white pinstripes. They accompanied gold and red–patterned ribbons and ribbons decorated with red and white peppermint-style stripes. Eventually all American combat soldiers received a victory medal from the United States government, too. This one hung from a rainbow-colored ribbon. Metal clasps adorned the ribbon to denote key battles from the individual's service. Conroy had participated in five noted battles, so his ribbon bore five battle clasps: Defensive Sector, Champagne-Marne, Aisne-Marne, St. Mihiel, and Meuse-Argonne.

All these awards prompted Conroy to confront this question: What should he do with them? Circumstantial evidence supports only one answer: He gave them to Stubby. Sometime during the war, consciously or unconsciously, Conroy had begun cultivating the persona of a war hero for his four-legged friend. He may have figured there was no better way to recognize his distinctive companion than to let him share in the war's rewards. Today Stubby's jacket is arrayed with a full complement of military medals and other souvenirs. No comparable booty was passed down to Conroy's descendants; there is only the one surviving cache of medals between the two wartime friends. Such an act

Robert Conroy and Stubby posed for a formal military portrait in France after the war ended. Eventually Stubby's uniform would hang heavy with their shared medals.

of generosity would be in keeping with Conroy's self-effacing character, and it reinforces the assertion that Stubby really did help Conroy survive the war.

This theory about the absence of a duplicate set of medals calls into question one of the central threads of Stubby lore: that he personally had earned all that recognition. In truth, with a few exceptions—such as the German Iron Cross and the Joanne d'Arc medallion presented while the pair was stationed near Neufchâteau—Stubby probably had not. Early on, the people around them likely understood this distinction. As the dog's fame began to grow, this technicality faded in importance. When his medal-heavy jacket drew more and more comment, Conroy would have had no reason to parse the details with news reporters and other admirers. To him, Stubby really *had* helped earn those medals, so there was no duplicity in letting his friend quite literally bear the rewards. Thus, over time, implications—such as Stubby having been personally decorated by the French government—grew into "facts."

Stubby's U.S. military insignia are a different matter, though. From the beginning, the mascot's jacket sported YD patches on its "shoulders." After the war his coat gained a wound stripe and three gold service chevrons, too. (Each of the fabric chevrons represented six months of overseas service.) These badges were sewn onto the "sleeve" area of the jacket, in keeping with Army protocol—the right sleeve for the wound stripe and the left sleeve for the service chevrons. Conroy's uniform would have displayed all these required trimmings, too, so he would have had to acquire a special set for his friend to keep the dog's jacket up to date and official.

It's easy to imagine that Conroy, especially as a member of the regimental headquarters company, would have had no difficulty obtaining such emblems. Undoubtedly he would have known the staffers who issued these honors, and these coworkers would have known the division's mascot. Fans of Stubby—and clearly these were legion—would have felt no compunction about dispensing the official decorative accoutrements for the likable dog.

That Stubby was becoming famous seems hard to dispute. Newspaper articles from the postwar era claim he had become a recognizable figure wherever he traveled in France, stopped on the streets by citizens and Allied soldiers alike. He was intimately acquainted with members of the 102nd Infantry Regiment and, because of Conroy's workplace mobility, had traveled widely throughout the 26th Division. Many accounts refer to him as the division's mascot; some even characterize him as the mascot for the entire American Expeditionary Forces. When Conroy started his scrapbook for his friend, he matter-of-factly had the album's leather-bound cover embossed with gold letters: "STUBBY A.E.F. MASCOT."

Stubby wasn't the only mascot to have made it through the war. Fanny the goat was alive and kicking, or at least butting, over in Company K. Philly, the stray pup adopted by the 315th Infantry Regiment, had survived, reportedly giving birth to four puppies along the way. Rags was even more raggedy by war's end, having lost part of an ear and the sight in one eye from a Meuse-Argonne gas attack that, unfortunately, led to the death of his adoptive soldier from the First Division. Cher Ami, although technically not a mascot, had become famous after delivering that last-hope message from the Lost Battalion. The pigeon survived the war but was minus most of one leg due to wounds received during its noteworthy flight.

Such fame helped these animals survive the peace, too. Other combat creatures were not so fortunate, even those that made it to Armistice Day. Most of the draft animals were sold, butchered, or destroyed, worn out by constant warfare. The vast majority of carrier pigeons were sold as well, although one postwar account claims that 500 of the most distinguished American birds were brought back to the United States and liberated in the riverfront parks of Washington, D.C. The Allied corps of service dogs was presumed too traumatized by combat for repatriation; thousands were euthanized.

In early 1919, the Yankee Division moved another step closer to home when the troops transferred from Montigny-le-Roi to an area near Le Mans, southwest of Paris. This time they didn't have to walk there, but the trip in 40 & 8 boxcars was so lengthy (more than three straight days of rail riding) and the accommodations so unpleasant (crowded together in unheated cars with no hot food and monotonous cold rations) that the soldiers might have reminisced about fall hikes through blackberry-rich countryside. Upon arriving, the troops moved into billets around the small town of Ecommoy, site of the division headquarters.

The soldiers settled into a military routine that was designed to keep them from becoming too restless while they awaited their chance to ship out for home. Military drills took a play-ful twist as the various units trained for intradivision competitions in war-themed athletic contests, everything from gas mask races to tent-pitching contests, from bayonet drills to five-mile marches. They even hiked footballs down chains of hands, competed against one another in inspection drills, and faced off in soup wagon races. They engaged in traditional athletic events as well, from tug-of-war to American football, from soccer to box-ing. Such activities helped the weeks of waiting pass by.

But, even better, were the furloughs.

The troops took turns, 600 men at a time, dispersing on these two-week leaves. Conroy and Stubby missed the finale of the three-day military tournament. Instead, on March 13, they set off on their last furlough tour of France. They didn't get very far. Soon after reaching Paris, Conroy became ill with the flu. He scrambled to figure out how to take care of Stubby even as he sought care for himself at a Red Cross hospital.

Conroy, who wrote up a dog-witness account of Stubby's life, notes that "Stubby had to plead his case" with the hospital staffers. Even when unwell, Conroy must have done a good job articulating the dog's sentiments. He reports in his narrative: "On learning Stubby's history the doctors went into a huddle and decided that Stubby could bunk alongside the soldier's cot in a tent on the hospital grounds. Stubby had no difficulty winning the friendship of everyone at the hospital. In fact, they wanted Stubby and the soldier to remain indefinitely."

That was all very well, but Conroy wanted to see the Mediterranean. As his companion "tells" it, "When Stubby let them know he had already used 8 days of a 14-day furlough and that he just had to see Monte Carlo, they agreed to release him provided he took good care of the convalescing soldier he was with." Even if Conroy's timing is off in the story (it would have been hard to travel in that era from Paris to the south of France and back in six days), it is clear that, yet again, his furry pal had won over another batch of fans.

Free (and healthy) at last, the pair headed south. The souvenirs that Conroy later pasted into Stubby's scrapbook give hints of their travels. They luxuriated in the dining cars of passenger trains. No 40 & 8s on this trip! They toured the seaside town of Villefranche-sur-Mer and saw the sites of Monte Carlo. If they entered any casinos, Stubby must not have placed any bets, for there are no souvenir receipts from any transactions. An uncaptioned photo in Stubby's scrapbook shows him swimming with Conroy in a large body of water. Could the image be from the south of France? Perhaps the pair sampled the warm waters of

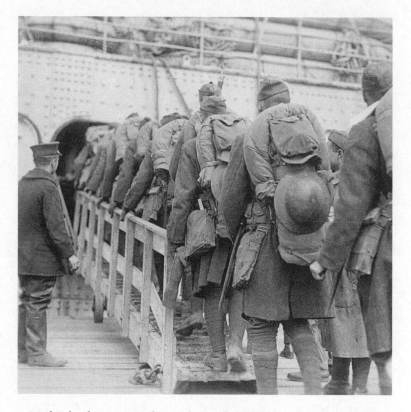

*Multiple ships carried members of the Yankee Division home,
just as they had done when the troops headed for France.
These members of the 102nd Field Artillery board the
Mongolia in Brest, bound for America.*

the Mediterranean, too, as part of their vacation? Any such fun
came to an end in time for them to return to their quarters south
of Le Mans on March 27.

After the two had reunited with their YD friends, Conroy
would have had to rush to repack their belongings. By March
31, they were on board the *Agamemnon*, bound for Boston. This
time Conroy did not have to smuggle Stubby onto the ship, at

least not exactly. As Conroy later wrote in his Stubby-narrated tale, "Although a number of Generals agreed that Stubby should be permitted to return to the U.S.A. they could not issue an order to that effect. They did suggest that Stubby might board the ship early with baggage. That was all Stubby needed."

Stubby and Conroy set sail from Brest with their entire 102nd Infantry Regiment. Somehow even Fanny the goat had made it on board. Together, men and mascots steamed west toward that setting sun and home.

S.C.269

Arrival at Commonwealth Pier, Boston, Mass., Troo*
"Formerly

PART THREE

HOMECOMING

The Agamemnon *delivered Robert Conroy and Stubby safely
back to the United States, arriving in Boston on April 7, 1919.*

May 1, 1919

★ ★ ★ ★ ★

Patrons line up to take seats at Poli's Bijoux Theatre, even for the weekday matinee. Voices buzz toward concentration as the lights dim. Newfangled entertainment shares the stage with vaudeville at its prime.

Singing. Dancing. Barrels of laughs.

Plus the frames speed past in Mary Pickford's new silent photoplay, Capt. Kidd, Jr. *Buried treasure. A protective grandfather. A winsome heroine. A hopeful suitor hanging on tenterhooks with the audience until the film draws near its end. Love requited at last.*

Stage lights illuminate Walker and Texas as they rope trick and dance their way across the boards. Ryan and Healey coax laughs from the crowd with humor and song. Visiting veterans from France, billed as Le Poilu, add their chansons to the program. More tunes. It's Nora Norrine, "the singing comedienne . . ."

More, more, the audience wants more. And so, added to the bill is a stump-tailed war hero, Stubby. The war dog who saw it all.

Imagine the scene.

Conroy, wearing his uniform, takes to the stage accompanied by his medal-bedecked companion. "An aggressive bull terrier," warned the promotion. This dog is unrestrained. Is he safe? Is he trained?

No doubt about it. Stubby goes through his moves. He can parade on command, turn left, look right, stop as directed. Conroy speaks for the dog. His words form a story that hangs heroically over the crowd. Smuggled to France. Off to the front. Survived four offensive campaigns. Wounded. Gassed. Captured a German, single-muzzledly. Decorated and feted. Here on parade.

Does the dog exhibit his signature trick? Undoubtedly. Salute, signals Conroy. Down goes the rear end. Up rises the head, the chest, the right paw. Higher and higher it goes until it brushes the right eye with great solemnity.

Applause. Surely there is applause.

Applause and cheers. A few tears for the soldiers who did not make it home.

A wave of patriotic pride.

What a war. What an act. What a show.

What a dog!

★ CHAPTER NINE ★

STATESIDE

INALLY, AFTER ALL THOSE MONTHS OF HESITANT PROGRESS, something happened quickly. The *Agamemnon* crossed the Atlantic more than three times as fast as the ship that Robert Conroy and Stubby had taken to Europe. One week the doughboys bid goodbye to the shores of France; the next they were sailing into Boston Harbor. The boat arrived on a dreary afternoon, Monday, April 7, 1919, emerging from fog to find an enthusiastic crowd of well-wishers. Family members and friends waved flags. Banners shouted slogans of greeting to loved ones. Arriving soldiers, eager to see the scene, lined three tiers of deck railings, stood in the ship's suspended lifeboats, hung from rigging, and even climbed the ladders on its smokestacks.

Governors of three states showed up to welcome back the region's own. The dignitary who stirred the Yankee men most, though, was the one who had been pulled from their midst during the darkest days of the Meuse-Argonne campaign: Maj. Gen. Clarence R. Edwards. Lusty yells commingled with hearty cheers of "Daddy, Daddy!" as word spread among the soldiers that their trusted leader was on hand. "It is evident that General Edwards is the idol of the outfit," observed Governor Marcus H. Holcomb of Connecticut.

The burst of speed that had propelled the doughboys home-ward dissipated upon arrival into the more typical hurry-up-and-wait style of their previous progress. It took hours to dock the ship. Furthermore, the men knew that any dockside reunions would be brief: The Army wasn't done with them yet. Demobi-lization would take weeks to complete, and the division would be sent to cool its heels at another encampment while members waited for the machinery of war to finish winding down.

First, though, the men could drink in the cheering hometown crowd. When it finally came time to go ashore, Stubby, according to Conroy, "marched off proudly in full regalia." No more sneak-ing around for this veteran! Stubby's arrival inaugurated a new phase in the dog's notoriety: press coverage. A correspondent for the *Hartford Courant* had spent time on board the *Agamemnon* before the troops disembarked, and the reporter filed a special dispatch in the next day's paper. "Mascots Include Dog and a Goat," read the headline. "Stubby Made Round Trip—But Fanny Butts," the subhead added.

The reporter employed a pattern that would repeat itself in countless news stories for the rest of the dog's life. Introduce a bit of tongue-in-cheek humor: *"He would have expressed him-self in the terms he usually used—simple enough but expres-sive—he might have wagged his tail, but there wasn't any to wag . . ."* Dazzle with a few remarkable details: *". . . and where his tail ought to have been hung an iron cross."* Slaughter the dog's personal narrative by blending fact with fancy: *"He was in every battle* [of the Yankee Division, mostly true], *but the French gas mask first made for him wouldn't fit, and another was never procured* [definitely false, and even illogical, which even the reporter immediately admits]. *How he avoided being gassed is a miracle."* Indulge in a bit of anthropomorphizing, perhaps aided by Conroy himself: *"According to his owner,*

Stubby is in favor of some kind of a league of nations for he doesn't want the dogs of war loose on the world again."

Stubby and his fellow doughboys spent the next few weeks at Camp Devens, about 40 miles west of Boston. Here, finally, they parted with the last of the lice that had hitchhiked their way through the war. They gained brief leave passes so they could visit

Robert Conroy and Stubby returned to the comforts of passenger trains after departing France. The pair traveled together extensively following the war.

family—Conroy made a trip with Stubby to New Britain—and they participated in a mix of paperwork, parading, and commendation. No doubt the men anticipated their discharge dates with a mixture of impatience and regret. Few bonds would ever be as strong again as the ones they had formed by literally going through a war together. With one another, there was an instant understanding, an unspoken common knowledge, and a shared wonder—my God, did we really do all that? They would return to civilian life ever altered, always an invisible step or two out of sync with colleagues and loved ones who respected their service but, really, had no clue what it had meant to come through the Great War.

The veterans shared one last blaze of glory, though, before they scattered to the forests, fields, hilltops, coastlines, and cities of New England and beyond. They had a parade. In fact they probably had several because home states and hometowns organized celebrations, too, after the Yankee Division splintered and subsets of local boys came home. But the biggest, grandest parade of all took place while they were still members of the U.S. military, and it took place through the heart of New England: Boston.

Stubby, no stranger to parades, earned a place of honor at the afternoon event, accompanying the color guard for his own 102nd Infantry Regiment. He knew the drill. Follow the flag bearers. Don't stray left or right. When ordered to turn "eyes right" at the reviewing stand, cock head to that side. At the next command, face forward again. Fanny followed farther behind, as part of K Company. In contrast to Stubby, the Kaiser's goat walked tethered to a soldier, presumably Corporal Simpson. She had already polished off the choicest parts of several hundred packed lunches while the parade formed up, and no one wanted her to stray to the sidelines for further snacking.

A million or more spectators lined the streets of downtown Boston for the event on April 25. Some 20,000 men passed in review, traversing most of the perimeter of the Boston Commons, rounding a corner of the public garden, traveling both directions on Commonwealth Avenue as far as Massachusetts Avenue, and then embarking on an even longer loop back to Massachusetts Avenue and then east again on Columbus Avenue toward the Commons and the dismissal point of Park Square. The route compared in length to one of the five-mile marches the dough-boys competed in during the closing games of their stay in France.

Temperatures dipped toward freezing, but the crowd hugged the route for hours, cheering incessantly. General Edwards him-self led the parade, astride a horse, holding his right arm in a salute for much of the distance, although he reportedly broke his formal stance when he reached his home address on Common-wealth Avenue; there he waved to his wife, who waved back from the front of their residence. Edwards was followed by staff mem-bers, a captured 220-mm German Howitzer, automobiles filled with wounded soldiers, the various military regiments, their color guards, their bands, and, of course, those marching mascots.

Demobilization followed within days. Conroy and Stubby left the Army on April 29. Conroy, as with other doughboys, received a discharge bonus of $60 (equivalent to about $800 today). Each departing soldier received a red discharge chevron, too. This fab-ric emblem, shaped like a fat, upside-down V, was to be sewn onto the upper left sleeve of a soldier's uniform to show that his military service had ended. Presumably Stubby drew no bonus, but he did acquire his own official discharge chevron, which was dutifully added to his uniform's left "sleeve."

On April 30, Conroy and Stubby paraded in Hartford with fellow Nutmeggers, as Connecticut residents have some-times been called, marching under sunny, warm skies before yet another appreciative hometown crowd. Once again Stubby walked behind his regimental color guard, and once again Fanny the goat followed several units back on a lead. Then the companies disbanded. Most soldiers headed for their hometowns. After the parade, Edward Simpson probably just walked with Fanny to his family home in Hartford. Conroy and Stubby, though, had a grander destination: the public stage.

While Conroy had been stationed at Camp Devens, Conroy's commanding officer had received a letter from a Mrs. S. Z. Poli of Poli's Theatrical Enterprises, based in New Haven. "You have in your company Corporal J. Robert Conroy," she wrote. "We are very desirous of securing the services of Corp. Conroy starting next Sunday, April 27th in connection with our local Victory Loan Drive." Mrs. Poli went on to ask if the corporal could be furloughed for a few days so that he could take part in the effort. She makes no mention anywhere in her letter of Stubby, but everyone seems to know, between the lines, that Conroy's dog was a crucial part of Mrs. Poli's vision. "We have prepared a very effective and, we believe, beneficial plan in which the services of Corp. Conroy are much needed," she explained.

Mrs. Poli's request advanced through two levels of review, according to the fading pencil notations that appear on the surviving document. "Can you give the Corp. up?" queries the second officer to consider the invitation. Apparently not, must have been the answer from the colonel he had contacted up the chain of command, or at least not in time for an April appearance. Mrs. Poli, unfazed, booked the soon-to-be-discharged corporal and his remarkable friend for a three-day engagement on her New Haven stage, starting on Thursday, May 1.

An unrecorded series of other bookings followed. Perhaps the pair appeared at other venues of Poli's Theatrical Enterprises—in Hartford, Springfield, and Worcester or Scranton, Bridgeport, and Norwich. If so, they had found a good gig. Stubby and Conroy each earned $62.50 for their first day's commitment in New Haven.

"Vaudeville demands Stubby's appearance," wrote Conroy
when he captioned souvenirs from their stage tour in
Stubby's scrapbook, including this flyer promoting an
appearance in New Haven, Connecticut.

Presumably they received the same for the three daily appearances they made on May 2 and May 3. Considering that soldiers had received $60 as their discharge-bonus following their lengthy military service, earning more than twice that (between them) for one day's work would have seemed almost unfathomable.

Sgt. John J. Curtin had even forecast such a future for Stubby in some of the concluding lines of his tribute poem: "When we take him back to the U.S.A., / Stubby will hold the stage, night and day." Conroy, though, eschewed the life of an entertainer. "The stage is a dog's life," he told a reporter in 1920. "Maybe Stubby could stand it, but I couldn't." After completing an initial tour of vaudeville stages, he and Stubby retired from the limelight to Conroy's hometown.

Conroy and Stubby moved into the new extended family house on Church Street, across town from his childhood neighborhood. As was the case with many veterans, Conroy tried to pick up with the life he had left behind before the war. For work, he turned to his former employer, Russell & Erwin Manufacturing Co., and they hired him as a traveling salesman. During the war the company had retooled to make weaponry, including gun parts and grenades. Now they resumed the manufacturing of door locks, latches, and other hardware for the builder's trade. Conroy began to travel and sell the company's wares.

For the first time in their nearly two-year-long friendship, Conroy and Stubby began to spend long stretches of time apart. While Conroy traveled, Stubby stayed behind in New Britain, settling into what may have been his first opportunity to enjoy a home setting. Conroy's eldest sister, Margaret, welcomed the dog's company while she cared for her two children. At first, she told a news reporter, "I was very much against his bringing Stubby home [from the warfront] because I was afraid that he would frighten my little three-year-old girl. But nobody could mind Stubby—he's a good beast—and the baby loves him a great deal—they are regular chums." Other family members reportedly enjoyed the dog's company, too.

Even though Conroy saw less of his friend, he didn't stop bragging about Stubby or run out of ways to have him honored. He was a salesman after all, and he knew how to combine those skills with his affable personality into a homespun pitch suitable for newspaper reporters and public figures alike. His first success could easily have been an accident. One can imagine what transpired when Conroy visited the YMCA in Hartford soon after his discharge. Perhaps his original intent was to obtain a postwar membership for himself in an organization that had provided warfront support to Army soldiers.

Stubby in tow, Conroy would undoubtedly have recounted the dog's catchy history, just as part of a friendly conversation. He and staffers may have joked that the dog, too, deserved one of the postwar memberships that were being offered to returning soldiers and, for the fun of it, they actually issued him one. Actually they did one better: They gave Stubby a life membership card. (The offer for human veterans was for three months of privileges.) Stubby earned a few extra perks, too. His "War Service Membership" was "Good for Three Bones," daily. And it included "A place to sleep," when the dog needed a home away from home.

The veteran and YMCA staffers may well have viewed the issuing of the card as a publicity stunt that would benefit the group's campaign for new members. Conroy would presumably have been happy to support the organization, and he clearly liked attaching honors to his beloved friend. Surviving records support this line of logic, starting with a story that ran during May 1919 in the *Hartford Courant*. The clipping shows a photo of Conroy, squatting beside Stubby, with the dog's new YMCA card pinned temporarily to his military uniform. A few days later Conroy received a letter from the Hartford Y's local administrator enclosing a copy of the photo and a report that the paper had "printed a cut of this about six inches square on their editorial page." Before signing off, he added: "Give Stubby my best regards and tell him his three bones are waiting for him."

Stubby's YMCA card became part of the mascot's signature story. Indeed, it helped to mint that story. One honor led to the next. Each publicity gesture triggered a new invitation of support. Victory Loan drives. American Red Cross membership campaigns. Support for the venerable Veterans of Foreign Wars. Participation in the newly formed American Legion for veterans of the Great War. Stubby became iconic, a symbol of the pluck, and fortitude, and modest pride of the boys who had crossed an ocean against steep odds and returned victorious. In short, the news media ate him up.

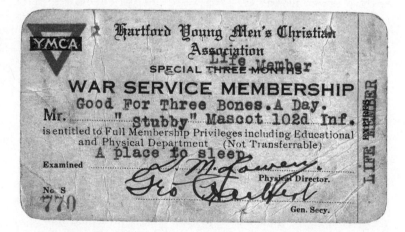

Stubby's membership in the YMCA "gives him the coveted privilege of sleeping in the lobby and getting three square bones a day from the Y.M. kitchen below," reported the Hartford Courant *when it announced the mascot's award.*

Stories began to appear locally at first, and later on in the national press, multiplying as prodigiously as trench lice. "Most Decorated Dog in A.E.F.," *Jacksonville Courier* in Jacksonville, Illinois (May 1921). "Stubby, Dog Hero is Honored Again," *Washington Post* (July 1921). "Stubby, 102d Mascot, to be Guest at Christmas Dinner," *Hartford Courant* (December 1922). "Hero Dog Hotel Guest," *New York Times* (December 1922). "Greatest of War Dogs to Attend Big Game," *Washington Post* (November 1924). "Stubby, the Canine Hero of the A.E.F.," *Washington Post* (November 1925).

Conroy pasted story after story into Stubby's scrapbook, adding items from the *Denver Post*, the New Orleans *Times-Picayune*, the *Chicago Daily Tribune*, the *Kansas City Star*, and the *Evening Bee* of Omaha, among many others. Occasionally he would correct a fact by adding an inked annotation to the clipping, but even then he only updated details about his personal military history (such as an erroneous attribution to his having served in the 102nd Field Artillery instead of its Infantry). Otherwise he seems to have celebrated the arrival of each story—whether accurate, embellished, or downright erroneous (even an article that credited Stubby with being female)—with equal enthusiasm and a dose of glue.

News reporters recycled details about Stubby's life until his printed bio was a tumbled mix of fact and fancy. No less venerable a paper than the *New York Times* explained to its readers in 1927 that the dog had earned his nickname because, "in the World War part of a leg was shot off, which accounts for his name," despite obvious proof to the contrary. Other stories presented him as a Marine instead of an Army veteran. Still others misidentified him by such names as Stubbie, Stuffy, and Hubby. Basic facts became distorted, as in a report of how he "was smuggled aboard the big transport at Hoboken by a squad of husky doughboys," listing not only an incorrect account of Stubby's departure but placing him at the wrong port, too.

Some reporters invented fanciful backstories for the famed mascot: "In his youth Stubby was a prize-winning dog at all the shows in New England, but he forgot all those days of triumph when Uncle Sam called his young men to arms." This same reporter went on to credit the war dog with unimaginable feats of survival. "That all was not plain beer and skittles, however, is shown by the fact that Stubby was wounded twice in battle. He accompanied his doughboy friends wherever they went, even if it meant attacking the enemy. That is how he happened to stop two bullets."

Another article published at about the same time commingled identical language with an even greater misrepresentation of the facts plus the misstatement of the dog's name: "Stuffy was wounded five times in action," the reporter claimed. "He accompanied his doughboy friends wherever they went, even if it meant attacking the enemy. This is how he happened to stop five bullets. But he was a 'toughy' as well as 'Stuffy,' and he recovered each time." Such "facts" spread to other accounts, and the misinformation, myths, and threads of truth continued to commingle, evolve, and reproduce in perpetuity.

Newspaper reporters laced their Stubby stories with humor and playful puns, describing "his hangdog look" at the thought of being left behind when the troops headed for France, or predicting the "howling success" of a dog show where he was slated to appear. Journalists made fun of his missing tail and offered anthropomorphic projections onto his thoughts. For example, a 1926 tribute in the *New York Times* noted, "Early in life Stubby longed for a career. Realizing the value of education, the brindle and white 'bull terrier' abandoned his nomadic life for that of a student. Selecting Yale University as his alma mater, he was soon recognized as a prodigy." But war broke out and the unusual scholar faced a tough choice, according to the writer. "Stubby came to the conclusion that he ought to do his bit for his country . . . [I]n such a time, when men were parted from mothers and wives to defend the honor of Uncle Sam, was he, a mere wanderer without dependents, to think of self?"

Reporters frequently resorted to hyperbole as a way to sum up the mascot's significance. The *Washington Post* suggested, for example, that Stubby "is probably better known and loved by more people than any other dog of his time," adding, "he is undoubtedly the most decorated dog in the world." A local Connecticut paper may have summed it up best: "Stubby is the most 'writ' up dog in America."

Stubby's popularity coincided with a growing increase in the adoption of dogs as pets. For centuries dogs had worked for their owners—as shepherds, as hunters, as sentries—and, with the exception of nobility, their owners had, as often as not, left them to sleep outside of their masters' house doors. That tradition began to change during the 19th century with an increased focus on the breeding and judging of dogs. Over time, show breeds gained popularity as house pets, and the owning and training of dogs became a middle-class hobby and not just an upper-class luxury.

Dogs such as Stubby, Rin Tin Tin (another World War I veteran, albeit as a puppy, rescued by an American soldier in France), and, later on, the fictional Lassie captured the public's fancy. Audiences marveled at the dogs' ability to perform what seemed like unusual feats, whether saluting or acting or rescuing someone—or even just sitting on command. Everyday folks wanted to own a dog for a pet, too.

German shepherds, collies, and Boston terriers became popular breeds, along with Airedales, beagles, bulldogs, and cocker spaniels. In fact, the Boston terrier, the breed with which Stubby holds an obvious kinship, reigned as either first or second in popularity according to the American Kennel Club for a 30-year span, beginning in 1905. The pet food industry was born, and the general public displayed a perennial appetite for dog stories, dog movies, dog shows, and all other things dog.

Stubby's media splashes became outsize exceptions to the everyday quiet that surrounded Conroy and his friend at their New Britain home base. The pair's bond remained strong in spite of Conroy's travel schedule, and the well-loved dog surely appreciated the predictable comforts of friendship, food, and shelter that filled his days. "He's just like a spoilt baby," Conroy told one local reporter who stopped by to interview him in 1920 for a story about three war dogs that had settled in Connecticut. The reporter, Bab Vickrey, documented one of the few surviving accounts of Stubby's downtime behavior. She observed how "he will cuddle down against a person, and when his back is rubbed he will growl gently—as nearly as he can make to a 'coo.'"

Vickrey led with Stubby in her *Bridgeport Herald* feature, adding companion stories on the other dogs. Tuck, a captured German shepherd, reportedly understood commands in three languages: German, French, and English. His final wartime owner, an American medical corps doctor, had trained him to deliver medical supplies and messages. Toute de Suite, an adopted French Pomeranian, suffered from exposure to poison gas and spent the rest of the war riding shotgun with his ambulance-driving owner.

Interestingly, Vickrey includes a comment in her feature about Conroy, pre-Stubby, that seems at odds with the historical record: "Bob never did like dogs," she reports, "wouldn't have one about the place. But Stubby won his heart entirely. And so they became confirmed chums." Could this be true? Is it possible that Conroy was not a dog person until he found himself charmed by Stubby? Readers are left to wonder if this statement, never repeated elsewhere in the historical record, has a ring of truth. No other interviews of Conroy survive, and Vickrey's account is otherwise accurate. If Conroy wasn't a fan of dogs before Stubby arrived, he'd certainly fallen for one in 1917.

When the Eastern Dog Club announced in early 1920 that it would, for the first time, recognize dog heroism as well as breeding, Conroy nominated Stubby for its inaugural award. "Eligible to this class are any dogs which have saved human life or which by their faithfulness have averted danger to human life," explained the club. "The dog that saves children or others from drowning or that scares away the burglar will have consideration." One such entrant, Prince, a mixed-breed burglary foiler, did receive commendation alongside Stubby. But Stubby's entry must have overwhelmed the judges with its overlapping themes of bravery, patriotism, and devotion. *What a dog! What a hero!* "He's probably a mutt," one judge reportedly said, "but he's done more than all the rest [of the show dogs] put together, and he shall have a medal."

Later that spring, probably as an additional gift from the dog club in conjunction with the promised medal, Stubby gained a special harness that highlighted his distinctions. The ornate dark leather device buckled under Stubby's chest, and it gleamed with small brass plates. Each oval disc bore a detail from the mascot's history, starting with the basics: "Stubby / Mascot / Yankee Division / New Haven, Conn. to France / 1917-19." Other plates ticked off the places Stubby had served (Chemin des Dames, Seicheprey, Toul, Château-Thierry, St. Mihiel, Verdun, Meuse-Argonne) and where he had traveled (Paris, Monaco, Nice, Monte Carlo). One prominent panel proclaimed Stubby's latest triumph: "Decorated by Eastern Dog Club, Boston, April 1920." Other brass tags conveyed his military pedigree, including a military service number (identical to Conroy's), a rendering of the Yankee Division "YD" logo, and three-dimensional representations of the wound stripe and trio of service bars that Stubby had received.

Veterans of the Yankee Division crowded around Stubby (with
Robert Conroy squatting beside him) and General "Daddy"
Edwards (behind the mascot) during one of their postwar
reunions. In 1922 the general sent Stubby a cordial letter at the
Carry On Club thanking him for sharing "your fine photograph."

The elaborate harness was fashioned so that Conroy could
mount a tiny, toy-size flag into position over the dog's back. So
outfitted, Stubby, too, became a flag bearer when he walked in
the company of a military color guard. On such occasions, he
sometimes appeared bearing a United States flag; other times
he paraded with a slightly larger banner that reproduced the
flags of the war's Allied countries. Sometimes Conroy displayed
a large silver medallion in place of the flag mount; most likely

this ornament was the hero medal promised to Stubby by the Eastern Dog Show judges, and it makes sense that they gave him the harness to display it, hence the brass tag notating his additional decoration by the club.

Stubby, looking more the hero than ever, began making the rounds with Conroy to various veterans reunions. They attended the national conventions of the American Legion, starting with the debut gathering in Minneapolis during November 1919, and they attended local and regional reunions of their Yankee Division brethren. There was Seicheprey Day to commemorate every April, parades timed to coincide with patriotic holidays, reunions at regional vacation spots, social gatherings at local veterans halls.

161

The old mascot fell right back into step, literally, whenever he met up with his fellow doughboys, and he could be counted on to lead any parade. His veteran friends enjoyed the chance to connect with their wartime pal, and strangers quickly made his acquaintance by shaking his paw. No doubt Stubby dutifully returned salutes as demanded, too. Such engagements weren't just rote reactions to circumstances; the dog liked the familiarity and attention of it all. As one reporter observed, when covering a veterans' gathering in the New Haven area, "Stubby seemed to be glad to meet former comrades as they affectionately patted him and called him by name."

The fun of reunions aside, by the fall of 1920 Robert Conroy had discovered what many veterans discovered after the war: Coming home could be complicated. Even the soldiers who had survived with limbs and lungs intact could find it no easier to slip back into an old way of life than it would have been for a snake to sheath itself in a shed skin. The person inside had been places, seen things—that old skin wasn't a natural fit anymore.

Conroy was making decent money as a traveling salesman for Russell & Erwin ($1,800 a year, plus expenses, or about $24,000 today), but higher ambitions or intellectual curiosity or general restlessness—or all three—made him want more. He'd seen the world, and he wasn't scared of it. So Conroy thought big, and, at age 28, he set his sights on law school. Then he packed up his things, beckoned to Stubby, and together they caught a train bound for Washington, D.C.

★ CHAPTER TEN ★

TOUCHDOWN!

They called themselves the Carry On Club, and, by default, Stubby became their unofficial mascot. By late summer 1920, he and Conroy had settled into a communal living space with a group of other veterans at 1600 Rhode Island Avenue, in northwest Washington, D.C. The men borrowed an old military command when they named themselves, perhaps representing their intention to carry on with their lives now that the war was over. The extent to which they may have carried on in today's playful meaning of the phrase is unrecorded. Conroy didn't smoke or drink (this was the era of alcohol prohibition, after all), and it's quite possible that even at their silliest the residents' carrying on remained pretty innocent. Stubby would have fit right in.

Conroy directed his forward momentum toward obtaining a law degree, and he gained admission, starting in the fall of 1920, to the law school of Catholic University in northeast Washington, D.C. It's unclear how he financed his education—perhaps with the vaudeville windfall; or through savings from his military service or postwar employment; or by qualifying for vocational training through a new federal program for wounded veterans.

He pursued his goal off and on for the next six years, following a nonlinear path that included pauses to earn money and enrollment at five different institutions.

While Conroy studied the law, Stubby pursued a new avocation, too: football. He made his debut on the gridiron that first fall, serving as the mascot for Conroy's own Catholic University. "Stubby's delight is chasing a football," reported the *Washington Post* during its preview of an upcoming contest with a school then known as Maryland State (part of today's University of Maryland). "There is no such word as down when he is chasing the pigskin," the paper proclaimed. Coach Harry Robb's Catholic Cardinals, with the media-anointed "wonder dog of the A.E.F." as its mascot, finished the 1920 season with a 5 and 2 record.

Stubby's fame grew around Washington, D.C., the way it had grown during the war—one bit of notoriety led to another until everyone seemed to know Stubby. For example, in March 1921, Conroy entered his friend in a showcase of Boston terriers. "Many service members shook paws with 'Stuffy' [sic], who seemed delighted with attentions shown him," noted one reporter. Stubby couldn't hold his own against the show's purebred dogs, but judges made sure the popular entrant received proper commendation anyway. Conroy barely had time to add a Kelly green–colored "Special Prize" ribbon to Stubby's scrapbook before more opportunities for fame materialized.

On March 4, 1921, Warren G. Harding had assumed the Presidency from Woodrow Wilson, a leader who, postwar, had lost both his health and his bid for the United States to sign the Treaty of Versailles and join the League of Nations. (In 1921, the United States signed separate treaties with Germany and other wartime combatants, officially ending the Great War.) Harding's arrival brought not just a change of party to the White House; it introduced a First Pet to the scene, too, Laddie Boy the Airedale.

*During the Humane Education Society parade in May 1921,
Stubby served as "guard of honor" for the young girl who
accompanied him, Miss Louise Johnson. This daughter
of an Army colonel appeared somber—or perhaps awestruck—
seated beside the canine war hero during their travels
down Pennsylvania Avenue.*

The Humane Education Society promptly tapped the new dogs
in town—Laddie Boy and Stubby—to headline an upcoming animal parade.

The President's dog, naturally, led the May event, riding on
a float pulled by six prizewinning horses. Eleven more floats
followed, including one bearing the medal-bedecked Stubby,
dressed in full regalia, with a U.S. flag rising from his harness.
Marching bands enlivened the accompanying menagerie of par-
rots, bulldogs, police dogs, goats, horses, and other assorted creatures. Additional parade stars included Peggy, a sheepdog who
had become a celebrity during war bond fund drives; a popular

Airedale known as Peter the Pirate, Jr.; General Pershing's famed horse Kedron; and Buddy the Bull, mascot of the Navy Yard.

Laddie Boy may have headed the parade, but Stubby earned top billing in their hometown *Washington Post* coverage. Papers from Illinois to Boston covered the event, too. "A World War hero passes in review before the President of the United States," explained a captioned photo in the *New York Times*. Before long, the Washington press corps was playfully portraying Laddie Boy and Stubby as rivals.

Whether or not the two dogs ever met is unclear, but Stubby did visit the White House a few weeks later when the First Lady hosted a lawn party to honor wounded veterans. Stubby met President Harding at the June 8 event, too, marking his second such introduction to a commander in chief. News reporters dutifully noted that during Stubby's encounter with Florence Harding she "held his leash for five minutes." (Conroy clocked the interval at ten minutes when he recorded news of it in the mascot's scrapbook.)

Conroy's classes at Catholic University ended the same month as the Hardings' lawn party, and he signed up for summer law study at George Washington University. Schooling may have usually come first, but he didn't let his academic duties prevent him from traveling to Boston for an Independence Day reunion of Yankee Division troops. The three-day program culminated, naturally, in a parade. Once again General Edwards led the procession, albeit with only 7,000 participants in his wake. Stubby, of course, was among the marchers, walking in his usual place of honor with the color guard for the 102nd Infantry Regiment. A tiny American flag fluttered over his back. "The dog marched in perfect alignment and with his head erect as though he realized his responsibility," reported one news account. "Many spectators uncovered for the tiny flag with as much respect as when the bigger banners passed."

No sooner had Conroy returned from New England than he prepared for an event of even greater magnitude. He and Stubby were to meet General Pershing himself, wartime commander of the A.E.F. and architect of the strategy that had helped to win the war, although with tremendous casualties. Conroy dressed in a three-piece suit and tie for the occasion; Stubby wore his military finest. Their orders were to meet the general in his private offices at the capital landmark known today as the Executive Office Building, then home to the Departments of War, Navy, and State.

The event, which Conroy characterized as "Stubby's greatest honor," received more space in his brief narrative memoir about his friend than did the dog's wartime service. Conroy recalled how Stubby's admission to the federal building was blocked initially when "he was told by guards that dogs are not allowed to enter." Writing from the mascot's point of view, Conroy adds, "Stubby quietly told them he was expected at the offices of the General of the Armies, John J. Pershing. After a telephone inquiry, the bar was removed and Stubby was escorted to Gen. Pershing's offices on the second floor."

News reporters and motion picture crews documented what followed: the pinning of a medal by Pershing onto Stubby's uniform. The Humane Education Society had created the award to commemorate his participation in its May parade and to recognize the mascot's bravery and service during wartime. Solid gold, the medal bore a likeness of Stubby, his name, the date of the parade, and other decorative motifs. Pershing, as a supporter of the organization, had been prevailed upon to present the award.

One press account states that the general ceremoniously "spoke a few words on the theme of 'man's best friend in peace or war,' and Stubby acknowledged the honor with a grateful bark." Another claims that, in reply, "Stubby merely licked his chops and wagged his diminutive tail." Photos show a uniform-clad

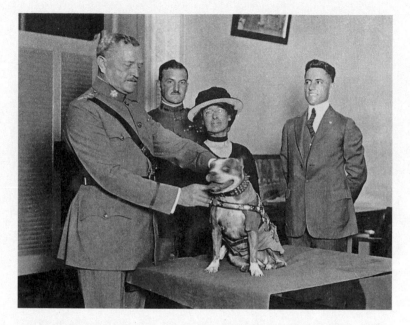

Robert Conroy beamed when Gen. John J. Pershing added a personalized medal to Stubby's jacket on July 6, 1921. Mrs. Clyde D. Parker, representing the award's sponsor, and a Pershing staffer attended the ceremony in the general's private office.

Pershing doing his best to look dignified while a dog sits in his office on a cloth-covered table. Stubby, ever patient with pomp and the press, simply pants. The general received a gold-trimmed leather wallet from the grateful organization in recognition of his much admired horse Kedron. The Hardings' Laddie Boy earned an honor, too, although his was not bestowed so formally. Stubby's award, reportedly, marked the first and last time Pershing ever pinned a medal on a dog.

Feature stories documenting the event appeared on page one of the *New York Times* and ran inside the *Washington Post*. The Universal Press news syndicate dispatched an account of the proceedings to its affiliated newspapers. Stubby's scrapbook includes multiple reports of the story—from Denver, from Newport News, from Hartford, and other locations. The wire story played up the rivalry between the big dogs of the nation's capital: "To prove that being decorated by the leader of America's victorious forces had left him the same old unpretentious Stubby, he barked a democratic greeting to Laddie Boy as he passed the White House on his return from the ceremony."

Not surprisingly, some people took exception to all the attention being showered on a mere dog. One correspondent penned a seething letter to the editor of the *Stars and Stripes* military newspaper. Pointing out all Stubby's recent honors, the author asks what the dog did during the war to deserve such recognition. "Nothing," he answers. "Absolutely nothing, but sneak along behind his master and wonder what the hell was going on . . . But did the dog have any idea at all where he was following his master to? No; and I'll say if he had he would have whipped his master and the whole company to keep from going . . . For this Stubby gets all those medals and the name, 'a real hero.' But the thousands of real heroes, the red-blooded American boys who left gallons of their blood and maybe an arm or a leg on the battlefields don't get these honors bestowed on them." The writer concludes, "If this Boston bull did so much and the boys didn't do anything, why not send an army of bull pups the next time and see who is entitled to these honors? I think the whole thing is nothing but a disgrace to the U.S. Army . . ."

Another correspondent pursued a different line of attack. "What a thrill runs over one," he noted sarcastically, upon learning of Stubby's YMCA privileges, "in these days of widespread unemployment, when innumerable ex-soldiers are starving in the streets of our big cities." Incensed by the dog's VIP treatment, the author caustically suggests that, "when the sad necessity arises, it would be only fit and proper for this historic animal to be buried with full military honors in the National cemetery alongside the Unknown Warrior."

Conroy, ever the optimist, interpreted such missives as a positive development for his invincible ally. He dutifully pasted the letters into his friend's scrapbook, then added his own interpretation to the comments. "Criticism of Stubby which proves he is famous," he wrote in white ink on the black paper, perhaps closing the book with a satisfying "thump." Nothing could tarnish Conroy's regard or enthusiasm for his charge. Elsewhere in the album he included a poem written by a fan named Margaret Shanks, seemingly one and the same as the respected war nurse and poet who had been an end-of-life caregiver to Susan B. Anthony. Shanks concluded her brief tribute with the stanza:

Stubby, doggie what a lesson
To us humans, you can teach
Humbly wearing regal honors
Lifts you just beyond our reach.

Taking both praise and put-downs in stride, Conroy kept his own goals in sight, too. In the fall of 1921, both he and Stubby shifted their athletic and academic allegiances to a new school, Georgetown University. Conroy would go on to gain the core of his law education at that institution. Because his studies at Catholic University and George Washington University represented the equivalent of one year of scholarship, Conroy entered Georgetown as a second-year law student. Meanwhile, Stubby became the mascot for the Hilltoppers, forerunners of the present-day Georgetown Hoyas.

As Georgetown's mascot, Stubby donned a gray uniform that sported a large blue "G." Then, during halftime, he repeated the pigskin pursuit that had entertained crowds at Catholic University. The Georgetown "Domesday" yearbook for 1923 features a full-page photo of Stubby—"B.S., M.A., Ph.D. Official G.U. Mascot"—that shows the dog in action. In the picture, a young male student, dressed like a sporty cheerleader, has just launched a football along the turf. He grins broadly as Stubby chugs after the ball, full throttle, preparing to butt it with his head. Thus launched, the football could, theoretically, stay in motion as long as the dog was permitted to remain on the field.

And so it went, game after game during Hilltopper halftimes, leaving football fans thoroughly entertained and fired up. It has even been suggested that Stubby's antics inspired the whole tradition of a halftime show, but such a claim is easier to make than confirm. More certain is that he at least established football traditions at Georgetown. Stubby's halftime routine became the model for the mascots who followed him, the early ones of which were, likewise, akin to Boston terriers. His immediate successor earned the nickname Hoya, already a popular expression as a school cheer, and several subsequent mascots were named Hoya, too. Eventually all those Hoya mascots and cheers triggered a migration toward referring to the whole team as the Hoyas instead of the Hilltoppers.

Stubby's tenure as Georgetown's mascot began in the fall of 1921 and continued off and on for the next several seasons, depending on Conroy's enrollment and residency. Even then, Georgetown football was a big deal. The dog entertained halftime crowds that regularly numbered in the thousands. Some home games were played on Georgetown Field; other contests took place at Griffith Stadium, the home field for the Washington Senators baseball team.

The Hilltoppers had finished their 1920 season with a 6-4 record that included an 80-to-nothing home-game shellacking of St. John's of Maryland and a 0-to-30 loss in Boston to Boston

College. The next year, aided by Stubby, Georgetown coach Albert Exendine stirred the Blue and Gray to an 8 and 1 record. In 1922, the Hilltoppers brought home six wins, lost three games, and tied one. The team traveled widely, playing such schools as Georgia Tech, Johns Hopkins, Lehigh University, Princeton, Virginia Tech, and Washington & Lee University.

The Georgetown eleven routinely played military football teams, too, including various regional Army outfits, as well as squads hosted by the Marines at Quantico. Sometimes those military outfits battled one another, too, and on one such occasion, in 1924, Stubby made a guest appearance opposite yet another press-manufactured rival, a Marine Corps mascot named Sergeant Major Jiggs. "Greatest of War Dogs to Attend Big Game," announced the *Washington Post* in advance of the contest.

Unlike Stubby, Sergeant Major Jiggs had not experienced wartime combat, having been born after World War I. This bulldog became the Marines' mascot in a nod to the moniker the corps had earned during the war, Devil Dogs, so named by their duly impressed German adversaries. The Marines loved their wrinkled, plump, admittedly ugly dog and, perhaps as an antidote to the fame of Stubby, pressed for Jiggs to receive official military rank. Such requests were reportedly granted on orders from two different Secretaries of the Navy, the first one making the animal a sergeant and, later on, a successor promoting him to sergeant major.

Thus Jiggs, technically, outranked Stubby, ignoring the fact that Stubby probably hadn't really been made a sergeant and, if period news reports are taken as a guide, was not even referred to as one during his lifetime. Terminology aside, Jiggs, too, had his own uniform, but, unlike Stubby's, his included a hat. Jiggs, however, exhibited no apparent skill on the football field, his chief talent seeming to be the fierceness with which he lunged from the end of his leash.

*Sergeant Major Jiggs, mascot for the Marines at Quantico,
"smoked a pipe at odd moments; and once in a while he took
a chew of Picnic Twist," reported the* Washington Post *in
its 1927 tribute following the eight-year-old bulldog's death.*

As the 1920s unfolded, Conroy somehow managed to juggle
law school, Stubby's football career, and their busy engagement
calendar of veterans' activities. Conroy would have been seen as
one of the lucky survivors of the war—all limbs intact, no lingering
consequences from being gassed, a roof over his head, undertaking
higher education, and so on. Not all Great War veterans were so
fortunate. After the parades ended, many former soldiers struggled to find work in a shrinking postwar economy. Unemployment

climbed from a wartime low of less than 2 percent to, by 1921, a high of 12 percent. The nation witnessed postwar race riots (with many African-American soldiers stunned by how they were shunted back into a system of segregation even though they'd fought on the nation's behalf for freedom and democracy). Inflation hit. A recession set in. Several fledgling federal agencies sought to meet the needs of veterans, but not until 1930 would they be consolidated into one Veterans Administration, and decades would pass before the government began to grasp the hidden scars of war and the level of support that veterans truly needed.

Veterans joined advocacy organizations, such as the American Legion, and attended local, regional, and national events where they could share their concerns and enjoy the camaraderie of fellow doughboys. Conroy and Stubby became regulars at the national convention of the American Legion, hitting Kansas City in 1921, New Orleans in 1922, St. Paul (one convention representing 1923–24), and Omaha in 1925. Each reunion brought Stubby and Conroy back in contact with old friends and lifted veterans' spirits. The dog's appearances in parades inevitably drew further media attention.

Stubby and Conroy kept up with their war buddies at a seemingly infinite number of local gatherings, too—in Washington, D.C., where Conroy helped to coordinate activities for local veterans of the Yankee Division; back home in Connecticut; returning with former doughboys to the Newport News, Virginia, site of their departure for Europe; and so on. The dog drew correspondence from General Edwards, sat on display during a 1922 Christmas dinner of Connecticut veterans, and, days later, broke the no-pets barrier at New York City's Hotel Majestic, which overlooked Central Park. The *New York Times* made note of the latter achievement, explaining that, "When Stubby's blanket, laden with medals and decorations . . . was exhibited, he was not only admitted to the hotel, but was given the best accommodations available and had a special chef assigned to attend to his gustatory desires."

Even in 1923, four years after returning home, many veterans continued to struggle with economic hardship. The American Legion began pressuring the government on their behalf for postwar assistance. Conroy felt allied enough with the cause to join the lobbying effort, and that meant that the famed A.E.F. mascot added his "voice" to the campaign, too. "Stubby is en route to Washington to make a Bonus appeal to President Harding on behalf of ex-service men," noted the text of a captioned photo of the dog. "He may make a bone appeal to the White House chef, afterward," observed the playful press account. The next year, Congress responded with a form of delayed gratification by authorizing the creation of life insurance policies based on individual service records. These policies held a limited immediate value as instruments for borrowing, and they could be redeemed in full, with interest, 21 years later, in 1945. Even that assistance helped, as did an economy that was finally on the mend.

By the summer of 1923, the 31-year-old Conroy had yet to complete his law school studies. So far, he had undertaken a year of coursework at Catholic University, a summer session at George Washington University, another summer session (this one at Yale University), one full year of studies at Georgetown, and one additional year at Georgetown that included unfinished coursework. Although his name remained on the books for the next school year at Georgetown, 1923–24, he completed no additional work. Instead Conroy took a job. A shortness of funds probably contributed to this change of plans, but so could the influence of an unlikely new acquaintance, a young employee at the Justice Department named John Edgar Hoover.

How well the two men knew each other is unclear, as is how they met, although it seems quite likely that they may have become acquainted through their law school connections. Hoover, for example, had earned his law degree from George Washington University in 1917, and the two may have met through interactions at that institution during Conroy's studies there.

Perhaps Hoover actively encouraged Conroy to apply for work as a Special Agent at the Bureau of Investigation, where Hoover served as assistant director. Conroy's war work in military intelligence served as an obvious credential for civilian work at the Justice Department's investigative wing. Conroy's application sped through processing when he submitted it on June 14, 1923. The acting attorney general sent Conroy an appointment letter on

Stubby and Robert Conroy (front row, third from left)
posed on the steps of Gibbons Hall at Catholic University
in this group photo, probably taken with fellow students
during his first year of law school, 1920–21.

July 9, even before all the reports were in regarding his references and background. Three days later Conroy signed the notarized oath that made him a special agent for the Bureau of Investigation. (This Justice Department division would subsequently be renamed the Federal Bureau of Investigation, or FBI.)

Documents from Conroy's FBI personnel file indicate that he was originally posted to the Hartford office of the Bureau. During the next 15 months, he served the organization in Mobile, Alabama, and in Minneapolis, as well. Conjecture is required to imagine what transpired during this period. Did Stubby travel with Conroy to these outposts? Or did he stay back in New Britain with family? Did the fellows at the Carry On Club ever watch over him?

Conroy left behind no definitive answers. Nor is it clear what had motivated him to seek such employment in the first place at that particular time. Did he think he would be able to stay in the D.C. area and continue his law studies on the side? Was he surprised to find himself posted to distant cities and moved around from site to site? Is it true, as is stated in a 1934 document in his file, that he requested a transfer to Washington, D.C., so that he could complete his study of the law? Or, as is stated elsewhere, that he requested an eight-month leave of absence to resume his studies? If so, that correspondence is missing from his file, presumably part of the 25 pages culled during a 1977 sweep of the records.

Questions remain unanswered, but one fact is clear: By 1924 Conroy wanted out. On October 11, 16 months after his appointment, he addressed a letter to Mr. J. E. Hoover, acting director, Bureau of Investigation. "Dear Sir," he began. "I herewith tender my resignation as Special Agent of the Department." Conroy reported that he had turned in his badge and other government property. Then, he signed his letter: "Very truly yours, J. Robert Conroy."

★ CHAPTER ELEVEN ★

AT EASE, SERGEANT STUBBY

B Y LATE OCTOBER 1924, ANY SEPARATIONS ROBERT CONROY and Stubby had endured during Conroy's service with the Bureau of Investigation were over. The pair returned to the Carry On Club in Washington, D.C., and Conroy went back to work on Stubby's résumé. During their extended absence from the nation's capital, President Harding had died, and that meant a new chief executive lived in the White House. Stubby had already crossed paths with Calvin Coolidge at least twice by then—in 1919 at the victory parade in Boston when Coolidge was the state's governor, and at the 1921 American Legion convention in Kansas City, which Coolidge had attended as vice president. Now Coolidge was President, and that meant Stubby needed to shake his hand in order to sustain his record of having met every President from his lifetime.

When Conroy requested a meeting between his famous friend and the newest U.S. President, the pair received an invitation to visit Coolidge at the White House. Before long, Stubby, decked out in his military uniform, met his newest commander in chief. Photos taken afterward on the White House lawn appeared in several publications and made their way into the mascot's scrapbook. Conroy's public relations campaign was back in business.

How old was Stubby by this time? His vagabond origins make it impossible to know for sure, but he could easily have been eight or nine by 1924, old enough to retire from football. "His fondness for butting the ball around the gridiron with his head was too much for his aging legs," the *Washington Post* wrote in the fall of 1925, explaining his absence from local stadiums. Conroy's ties to Georgetown had ended by then, too. He had left school in the spring of 1923 without completing his coursework and had officially withdrawn from the program in February 1924, while employed by the Justice Department.

After leaving the Bureau of Investigation, Conroy took a job on Capitol Hill and resumed his study of the law, switching schools one last time. It would take him two more years to earn his degree, but on June 12, 1926, at the age of 34, he graduated from National University Law School, a program later affiliated with George Washington University. His accomplishment had been almost six years in the making despite the long odds of short finances, changing enrollments, and career diversions. The next year he earned admittance to the bar of the District of Columbia.

Conroy worked on Capitol Hill for most of the rest of the decade, serving as a staffer for Representative Edward Hart Fenn, a Republican from Connecticut. Not only did both men hail from the Nutmeg State, the pair shared an allegiance to the same National Guard unit that had become Conroy's 102nd Infantry Regiment during the First World War. Both connections may have helped Conroy get the job; they certainly couldn't have hurt as he assumed the duties of secretary for the congressman. Later on he

Stubby at the capitol in Washington D.C.

Conroy placed objects into Stubby's scrapbook somewhat randomly, combining, for example, this photo of him and Stubby in Washington, D.C., with a 1921 letter from the Connecticut American Legion inviting "yourself and your famous Y.D. Mascot, Stubby, to attend our State Convention in Bridgeport."

served as clerk for the House Committee on the Census, which Fenn chaired. Fenn valued Conroy as a hardworking staff member, a man of excellent "character, reputation, and habits."

Stubby may not have accompanied Conroy to work every day, but he did visit the site, as is evidenced by photos in his scrapbook that capture him on the steps of the Capitol. There's Stubby standing alone, in profile, displaying the left flank of his uniform, his brass-tagged harness resting at his feet, his head turned dutifully in a front-facing pose. In a companion photo, all remains the same except that he has flipped position so that his right flank is highlighted. The dome of the U.S. Capitol rises behind him. Another image shows Conroy seated on the steps beside Stubby. The uniformed mascot stands at attention, his gaze focused stoically at some indistinct point on the horizon while Conroy, dressed in business attire complete with bowler-style hat, offers a modest smile to the photographer.

Conroy recorded one story in his memoir about Stubby that hints at the playful downtime the pair shared during their years in the nation's capital. He wrote, "One day when Stubby was near the Washington Monument, a friend [meaning Conroy] carried him under his raincoat past the guards and part way up the stairs. Stubby then walked to the top of the monument and after looking over the City of Washington, he walked down the stairs and passed the guards who could not understand how that dog got by them. Of course, they did not know it was a minor operation for Stubby."

Such frozen moments of time offer the slimmest hints of all the memories the friends must have made during their postwar years together. The photos, the newspaper headlines, the awards, the few paragraphs of remembrance—these artifacts capture one side of their relationship. But anyone who has ever loved a dog knows there would have been plenty of occasions where the two of them romped together, where Conroy provided timely care for his charge, where Stubby lifted Conroy's spirits without his companion even realizing it. There would have been countless moments where Stubby sidled over to his friend and Conroy obligingly reached down to pet him until he growled contentedly in that low, soft way of his that was akin to the cooing of a baby.

Stubby would have felt completely at home back in Washington, D.C., with Conroy. He had all the creature comforts he could want, combined with the company of former doughboys. Even after the pair moved on from the camaraderie of the Carry On Club, they remained connected within a tight network of Yankee Division veterans, many of whom had attained positions of prominence in the government. In addition to various military officers, the two were friends with the personal physician for the U.S. President; Representative William P. Connery, Jr., a Democrat from Massachusetts; Connery's younger brother Lawrence, who served as his congressional secretary and later filled his vacant seat; and Representative Carroll Reece, a Republican from Tennessee. All had served with the Yankee Division.

Conroy seemed at ease amongst this circle of well-connected friends. He may not have shared their ambitions for elected office, but he did pursue public service and held responsible posts on Capitol Hill. For years he had juggled a complicated calendar of work, study, and socializing with veterans—including at distant national conventions—all the while caring for a very popular war hero. He was forever managing social requests that revolved around Stubby. In late 1924, for example, his friend Congressman Connery invited them to an event for a new organization for local Yankee Division veterans. "We are counting on you being present and we also particularly want you, if you can, to bring Stubby, who, though we are inviting the General [presumably General Edwards], shall have a place of honor."

Meanwhile Stubby presented himself at a local fund-raiser for the Animal Rescue League, a group that counted First Lady Grace Coolidge as one of its patrons; showed up for an Easter egg roll; and made other public appearances upon request. By the time the pair visited the 1925 American Legion Convention in Omaha, they were old friends with countless convention guests, even President Calvin Coolidge. Stubby appears to have dutifully slipped in and out of his uniform as occasions required. Even as he aged, the garment still could be snapped shut around his belly, a feat that might have proven challenging to other maturing veterans. Medals and souvenir pins began to weigh down the soft chamois leather of the jacket, but Conroy never seemed to tire of finding new ways to have the old mascot honored.

"We raise corn; we raise beans; we raise hell in New Or-leens!"
chanted veterans from Illinois when they marched in the city's
1922 American Legion parade. Stubby invariably turned heads
when he paraded at such events.

In 1925 he helped arrange for Stubby to have his likeness painted by Charles Ayer Whipple, a noted portraitist in the nation's capital. According to news reports and a period photograph made during the work's creation, the artist originally envisioned a portrayal of Stubby amidst a combat scene from France. Whipple's final work, though, shows the war hero in a formal stance against a solid background.

Another surviving photograph documents that a female artist assisted with the creation of Whipple's painting. This image captures Stubby standing in one of his classic profile shots, left flank exposed, head turned toward the artist. During the session, he is literally posing astride his open scrapbook, but that detail has been omitted from the final rendering. So has Stubby's tongue, which, when the photo was snapped, hangs lazily from his mouth. For the finished work, the old mascot looks stoic, weary, loyal, wise, and dignified. No slobbery tongue in sight.

Early in 1926 Conroy contacted the American Legion's Eddy-Glover post back home in New Britain in pursuit of another honor for his friend. The post had considered Stubby an honorary member ever since it was founded. Now Conroy wanted to make it official. He typed up a membership application for himself and the old YD mascot, duly confirming having been "gassed Nov. 2, 1918, Bois d'Ormont." Conroy signed the application. Then he inked the bottom of one of Stubby's paws and affixed its print on the form. He added a four-dollar money order to the request and mailed it to Connecticut. Not surprisingly, both of their applications received approval. Stubby was officially a member of their hometown post.

Conroy had known his four-footed companion for the better part of a decade by the time he stamped that paw print on the American Legion membership application. Did he sense that his friend's life was coming to an end? Was that New Britain application one last reach for glory, or just the latest idea to emerge during his tireless pursuit of creative publicity? One is left to wonder: Had Stubby's tour of combat duty shaved some longevity from his life span? By 1926, could he still climb stairs? Could he still drop to his haunches, rear up from his front feet, raise his right paw, and salute?

There was a time when the veteran warrior could knock off a salute with ease. Called to duty with Conroy for a 1922 ceremony at the Eddy-Glover post in New Britain, Stubby had entered the American Legion hall under the attentive gaze of a local reporter. At first, the mascot "looked around, apparently bewildered," observed the writer. "Then, seeing the one thing that he recognized, he trotted soberly over to where the uniformed men were standing and reared back on his haunches in a perfect canine salute. Stubby had recognized the uniforms of his old buddies in France."

The journalist observed Stubby's attention to further cues, too. "When the solemn procession started on its memorial march, Stubby was in a back file, but as the drummers struck up their music, he left the rear, maneuvered about and finally finished the march at the very head of the procession, stopping with obvious understanding as the former soldiers stood at attention before each memorial pillar to attach a wreath in memory of some soldier or sailor."

During the war, Conroy had never known if he or Stubby would live through the next day of combat. Thoughts of mortality must surely have receded after the pair returned safely to the United States. By 1926, though, nine years into their partnership, with Conroy reckoning the mascot's age at about 11, he must have begun to wonder again: How many more years, or months, or even days did he have left to enjoy being with his friend?

The answer came that year at midnight on the 16th of March. Stubby, ever the game companion, couldn't push on any longer. He'd had enough. Of course the two were together, at home in

186

Conroy's apartment. How many times had Stubby kept watch over a dying soldier on the battlefields of France? Now it was his turn to go and Conroy's turn to hold vigil. When Conroy cradled the old war dog in his arms, did Stubby's stump of a tail signal his happiness one last time? Did their eyes connect in one final moment of parting?

If so, Conroy kept such personal memories to himself. He wrote sparingly about Stubby's death, simply referring to him, when he penned a brief obituary, as his "closest comrade . . . during the war and the years which followed." This notice helped spread the news to the mascot's legions of friends: Stubby was no more. He had gone west, in the parlance of the day, gone west the way of so many young men during the war.

"His passing on was a peaceful end to an adventurous life," reported Conroy, "and it seemed as though his last message was one of gratitude to all who had loved, and been kind to him." After "Machine Gun" Parker heard of Stubby's death, he replied, "Reunions will miss a thrill in old Stubby's loss, and he will be mourned as sincerely as any other of our comrades." General Edwards reportedly sent condolences, too.

Obituaries ran in the *Washington Post,* the *New York Times,* and countless other papers. Editorials were penned in praise of the dog. "The boys loved him and now that the tiny life is ended, a real link with the Great Adventure is snapped," observed a New Haven newspaper. The *New Britain Herald* extolled, "A dog is a dog, some folks will say . . . But there are times when a dog is more than a dog; when he has all the attributes of a human being, plus such undying love and affection as few human beings possess for anyone but their own kith and kin."

The writer, just warming up, continued: "Stubby only a dog? Nonsense! Stubby was the concentration of all we like in human beings and lacked everything we dislike in them. Stubby was the visible incarnation of the great spirit that hovered over the 26th."

Stubby's body barely had a chance to grow cold before Conroy began acting again on the war hero's behalf. Years earlier an affronted veteran had scoffed that the medal-wearing mascot would deserve to be buried in Arlington National Cemetery, and plenty of Stubby's fans would probably have championed that proposal. Conroy, however, had a different memorial in mind. He wanted to preserve Stubby— literally, physically preserve him— and keep his memory alive in a museum.

Such an action was not without precedent. Devoted fans of the Confederate war hero Thomas J. "Stonewall" Jackson had elected to stuff his horse when it died, thus preserving the trusty mount the general had been riding when he had accidentally been shot and killed by friendly fire in 1863. Winchester, the steed of Union general Philip Sheridan, had likewise been preserved, as had the dog Owney, a 19th-century mascot for the railway postal service. At life's end, someone had even stuffed the pigeon Cher Ami, for goodness sake. Why not Stubby?

Conroy contacted the Smithsonian Institution for help. A staff taxidermist prepared the mount to the museum's highest technical standards. The employee honored Conroy's request that the dog's perishable remains be cremated, sealed in an airtight metal container, and embedded within the plaster cast that supported his fur-coated exterior. The mounted mascot assumed his classic pose, of course, standing in profile with his head cocked toward the right, glassy brown eyes focused on the horizon, supported by "the four paws which carried him over the battlefields of France."

Some details of the dog were altered, of necessity, during this treatment. His dark muzzle gave way to a tastefully created white one. Stubby's ears were set attentively erect, giving him in death a more assertive appearance than he had actually presented in life, at least when photographed, for in most pictures he displays his ears submissively and endearingly flattened onto his head.

All these preparations would have transpired with understandable urgency following Stubby's death. The journey the dog took toward his final resting place, however, unfolded over many decades. On several occasions, Conroy stepped back into service on behalf of his friend, making it his personal responsibility to assure that the famed mascot of the old YD would never fade from memory.

At first, Conroy kept custody of the stuffed Stubby; sometimes he even brought him along to veterans' conventions and reunions. Stubby appeared on display in shop windows. News reporters wrote about the exhibitions. Conroy pasted the clippings in the dog's scrapbook. It was almost as if the old patterns were unbreakable.

In 1927, Conroy found a more permanent home for the Great War veteran and offered him to the American Red Cross Museum in Washington, D.C., on a long-term loan. Such an exhibition space made perfect sense, given Stubby's role as a rescue dog during the war. Fellow members from the Eddy-Glover post in New Britain chipped in for a plaque that could accompany the display. Conroy probably helped draft the remarks that Congressman Fenn, his boss and fellow veteran, read when the display was dedicated on December 7, 1927. Fenn's speech recounted all of Stubby's greatest achievements: Originated in New Haven . . . smuggled to France . . . wounded in battle . . . returned victorious . . . met three Presidents . . . decorated by Pershing . . . honored and loved . . . etc., etc. Stubby remained in the museum until 1941 when efforts related to the Second World War displaced exhibits at the Red Cross headquarters.

Soon after Stubby's death, Conroy had considered giving his preserved friend to the Smithsonian. Throughout the 1940s and into the '50s, though, the pair resided together again. In 1954, their quiet reunion was disrupted when fire broke out during the night at Conroy's residential hotel, the Chastleton, on 16th and R streets in northwest Washington, D.C. Firefighters arrived and ordered the building evacuated. When Conroy and Stubby emerged from the structure, the duo made headlines again. "Dog War Hero Safe," began the caption for a photo that was snapped as they exited. There they were, back in the news once more. Conroy, an overcoat thrown over his pajamas, stands at almost military-style attention in the published picture. He looks quite dignified, even with his mismatched attire. Stubby accompanies him, tucked safely under the man's left arm in a modified football carry. Conroy's forearm curls under the dog's belly and Stubby's legs dangle stiffly below, attached to an unseen pedestal mount.

A few months later, Conroy loaned Stubby once more to the American Red Cross Museum. When exhibit space became tight there yet again, Conroy turned to the Smithsonian for shelter. This time he parted company permanently from his friend. The gift took place on May 22, 1956, a few months after the 30th anniversary of the dog's death. At 64 years of age himself, Conroy may have felt it was time to put his Stubby-related affairs in order. He gave the museum not just the mounted mascot but the dog's scrapbook, his harness, his studded collar, and his medal-laden jacket, as well.

One can imagine that parting permanently from such treasures was bittersweet. By letting them go, Conroy knew Stubby stood a better chance of lasting fame. By letting them go, Conroy lost physical proximity to the friend who had helped him get through the war, to his companion after the war, and to the avocation that had provided him so much pleasure over the years. At least he must have been gratified to see his comrade go on display soon after, wearing his jacket and studded collar, inside a glass case at the Arts and Industries Building, next door to the landmark Smithsonian Castle.

Conroy's world didn't just stand still during the 30-year span between Stubby's death in 1926 and his arrival at the Smithsonian in 1956. A whole lifetime of events transpired, starting with his marriage in 1927 to Ruth M. Burghardt, a Connecticut native like himself, whom he had met through a capital city social club called the Connecticut State Society. Their courtship was brief and so was their marriage. Details of their parting are slim and uncharacteristically unflattering. Less than a year after their wedding, Conroy walked away from his marriage, leaving behind a pregnant wife and plenty of unanswered questions.

Even the grandchildren who eventually followed—the three sons and one daughter born to Conroy's only child, Elaine Virginia

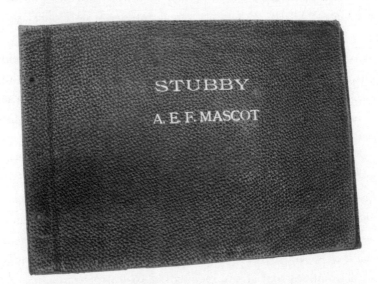

Stubby's scrapbook features ledger-size black pages. Robert Conroy added most items without comment, but occasionally he penned captions using white ink.

Conroy—inherited only the roughest sense of what had transpired prior to their mother's birth. What made Conroy unhappy in the marriage? Had he felt trapped by this early pregnancy? Did his years of life as a bachelor—he was 35 when he married—or even his rambling travels as a soldier and since, leave him unprepared for the realities of settling down? Had he realized that he'd made a terrible mistake by marrying? His ex-wife developed a reputation for being unusually eccentric, and years later even her own grown daughter broke off communication with the woman whom Conroy had likewise cut from his life. Had he just made a bad match?

Nearly a half century would pass before Conroy married again. Curtis Deane, his eldest grandson, learned of the second marriage in 1975 during one of the seasonal trips he made as an adult to visit his retired grandfather. "Meet Margaret," the 83-year-old Conroy reportedly said—and that was that. Conroy's relations with his daughter and, later on, with her own family evolved and improved over time. At first, father and daughter were estranged, although he reportedly kept track of Elaine's whereabouts through the help of friends from his days at the Bureau of Investigation. Elaine, an exceptional student, graduated while still a teenager from George Washington University, worked for the U.S. government, and married John Breed Deane, a fellow alum.

Their children—Conroy's grandchildren—have childhood memories of receiving cash each Christmas from the man they knew as Grandfather Bob. They remember him sending their mother money and perfume. Pets were plentiful in the Deane family home. Their father had a saying that the kids were "raised by dogs." Stubby lore added an extra dimension of authenticity to that claim, inculcating Conroy's grandchildren with a lifelong love of dogs. As the children began to come of age, their grandfather and their mother were reconciled, thanks in part to diplomacy conducted by Curtis Deane. As a result, Conroy's grandchildren had the chance to become better acquainted with the man who had himself come of age with a dog.

Conroy's career, as with his family life, took multiple and sporadically documented turns. His stint on Capitol Hill came to an end around 1928. Meanwhile, over a seven-year span starting in 1925, he made repeated attempts to return to the Bureau of Investigation as a special agent. Clearly his earlier post had meant a great deal to him, even though it had only lasted for a brief time. On four occasions—1925, 1928, 1931, and 1932—he sought to reenter the force. Some of the paperwork is missing from his FBI personnel file, but it's clear from the evaluation that accompanied his 1928 application that his truncated marriage weighed heavily against him in the consideration.

"Not qualified," reads the boldly scribbled notation on one key document. The initials J.E.H.—J. Edgar Hoover—follow. Hoover's broad strokes highlight the marriage and a few critical comments that accompany multiple testimonials to Conroy's upstanding character. Childhood friends. Prewar employers. Commanding Army officers. Congressman Fenn. Acquaintances from work. Accomplished veterans. None of those mattered on Hoover's scale of conduct. Neither did letters of support in 1931 and 1932 from such figures as Senator Hiram Bingham of Connecticut, other members of Congress, and the secretary to the U.S. President. "Beyond the age limit," reads one notation in the file concerning a 1931 query, the year Conroy turned 39.

So Conroy set aside his dreams of returning to the Bureau and pursued other lines of work. Certainly he practiced the law. He may have worked in the defense industry, as well. The Great Depression had begun following the 1929 crash of the stock market, and Conroy navigated its economic hardships along with the rest of the nation. He spent some of the following decades in

Washington, D.C., working for the Veterans of Foreign Wars as a legislative officer, for example, but he lived elsewhere, too, including Boston and outside of Baltimore.

When World War I veterans joined the ranks of those hardest hit by the Depression, their thoughts returned to their postwar bonuses. By 1932, plenty of families were so impoverished that it no longer seemed practical to wait for their bonus life insurance policies to mature in 1945. The down-on-their-luck veterans organized what they called the Bonus Army and the Bonus Expeditionary Force, playing off the name of the A.E.F., and in June they descended on Washington by the thousands with this plea: Pay our bonuses now.

To emphasize their determination, some 25,000 veterans and their family members set up an encampment on public land. It seems unlikely that Conroy would have joined such an act of civil disobedience, but he must have understood the desperation felt by his fellow doughboys. The federal government did not, however. A month after the occupation began, President Herbert Hoover ordered the U.S. Army to clear the shantytown. Fellow Great War soldiers Douglas MacArthur and George S. Patton were among the officers who matter-of-factly routed the squatters using bayonets, tear gas, and tanks. Then the troops burned the settlement to the ground. (Two infants died in the attack from the effects of the tear gas.)

Discouraged but not defeated, the veterans returned to the nation's capital the next year, hoping for a better reception from a new President, Franklin D. Roosevelt. No one threatened the protesters with bayonets this time, but their appeals still went unanswered. The impoverished veterans persisted annually in their plea until it was finally granted in June 1936, with a Congressional override of a Roosevelt veto. The long-sought bonuses amounted to about $550 per veteran, or just over $9,000 today when adjusted for inflation. They could be completely cashed, partially liquidated, or allowed to mature until 1945, collecting

3 percent interest. Most veterans elected for immediate payment, and the resulting infusion of cash served as an inadvertent and valuable source of Depression-era economic stimulus.

Perhaps Conroy collected some of his bonus and used it to fund his 1937 trip to Europe, returning home this time not on a troop transport ship but on the *Queen Mary*. If the 45-year-old veteran returned to visit battlefronts of the Great War, he brought back no surviving souvenirs. By 1937, not even two decades had passed since the end of the First World War, and yet in just two more years the next world war would begin. After the United States joined the conflict in 1941, Conroy and his brother, Hugh, both reported for duty. Family lore says that Robert Conroy served a role with military intelligence during this conflict, too, working stateside this time, but details are thin.

As the years unfolded, how often did the aging doughboy drop by the Red Cross Museum in Washington, D.C., and, later, the Arts and Industries Building at the Smithsonian to visit his old friend? Curtis Deane has youthful memories of being taken to the latter site by his grandfather to see the famed mascot. "He was very proud of Stubby," recalls Deane, noting that a Smithsonian staffer joined them for lunch as part of their visit.

Eventually Conroy retired to Palm Beach, Florida, as did his twin sisters. Their brother and elder sister Alice were frequent visitors. (Their oldest sister, Margaret, had died in 1957; Conroy outlived all his siblings except Alice, who died within three months of his passing.) Always the networker, even in retirement, Conroy kept in touch with aging veterans from World War I, and he joined the social club of the many former FBI agents who retired to south Florida. Conroy held sway in Palm Beach as a sort of de facto mayor, according to his eldest grandson. "He was a gentleman 20 ways to Sunday," Curtis Deane recalls, and had "a keen sense of humor." Deane notes that his grandfather "vehemently opposed discrimination," and he helped to break down local racial and anti-Semitic barriers. Although the aging veteran could still drive, he preferred to tour town by bicycle.

Six decades elapsed after Stubby's death, and yet Conroy never again owned another dog. Two wives, yes. But only one dog.

In the spring of 1987, at age 95, Conroy had a fall that landed him in the hospital. The accident coincided with one of Curtis Deane's annual spring visits. Deane learned about the injury only after his arrival, and he spent his vacation visiting the family patriarch at the hospital. He bid his grandfather farewell on April 25, 1987, and flew back to his home in New York. "I just knew I'd never see him again," he recalls. No sooner had he reached home than the news arrived of his grandfather's passing. Sixty-one years after Stubby's death, Conroy, too, had gone west.

"He was a proud man with a lot of dignity," recalls his grandson. Conroy hadn't spent time in a hospital since his 1919 stay in Paris for the flu, and he didn't want to languish in one at the end of his life. Deane believes his grandfather held on so that the two of them could be together one last time. According to the story shared by Conroy's second wife, her husband turned to her on that spring day, soon after his grandson's departure, and said, "Margaret, I've had enough. This is it. I love you very much. Goodbye."

Then the old warrior closed his eyes and died.

AFTERWORD

"WE INHERITED THIS STORY," EXPLAINS ALEXANDRA Deane Thornton, Robert Conroy's youngest grandchild and only granddaughter. Imagine that. Imagine growing up with Stubby, the iconic hero of World War I, as a chapter in your own family's history. He's not just a quirky figure you hear about once and forget. Instead of being a celebrity, he's one of your own. He's a mascot that a consoling veteran recollects at your grandfather's funeral. He's a story you tell to your own children, your nieces, your nephews. He's a topic you share with friends and a link to your personal past. He's the reason your grandfather left you that blue Samsonite suitcase, the contents of which you've gathered to review with fresh eyes and an interested author.

It takes a while to even find the material, long-since transferred to a storage carton. When we do, we unearth the treasures Conroy didn't give to the Smithsonian, the few links to his old friend that he saved to his life's end. Unpublished photos, including an unexpected image from 1917 taken at Yale before Conroy and Stubby shipped out for France. Conroy's official military discharge form, which answers key questions about his wartime chronology. The only surviving print I've seen of a frequently published publicity photo where Stubby stands balanced on a chair, front feet raised on its back rails, so that his jacket can be seen in overview.

We find confirmation that in 1933, seven years after Stubby's death, Conroy received a Purple Heart in delayed recognition for having been wounded during the First World War. (Other meritorious Great War veterans received the same honor about this time, too, as part of a celebration commemorating the bicentennial of George Washington's birth.) This military decoration with all likelihood corresponds to the one now pinned to Stubby's jacket, adding weight to the theory that many of the medals attributed to the mascot were actually earned by Robert Conroy himself.

The family history box yields other treasures and clues, as well. We find a Yankee Division beret that Conroy must have worn during veterans' parades, and evidence that he wrote that brief memoir about Stubby for the newsletter of the Society of Former Members of the FBI. We find the photo taken at Catholic University of Conroy with Stubby and fellow students. And we find more pictures. A framed montage of Stubby's most-published images. A few prints showing Conroy visiting Stubby at the Smithsonian. Photos of the aging veteran, his thick head of hair turned white but his trademark smile as bright as ever.

There are non-Stubby items, too. An old address book. Banking records. Christening cups that belonged to Conroy's twin sisters. But Stubby is a unifying theme. Imagine having such items filed alongside your other family history of births and deaths, graduations and marriages. When you inherit a story, it becomes a part of you till death do you part.

Curtis Deane, as the eldest grandchild, may have known Conroy the best of his three siblings, and he appreciated his grandfather's passion for the old YD mascot. One could even say he inherited that passion. In the 1990s, Deane helped rescue Stubby from a long-term-storage banishment that had followed a

*Although Robert Conroy gave the Smithsonian most
of the artifacts from his years with Stubby, he held on to
a few mementos from their friendship, including this postwar
publicity shot. The mascot's Iron Cross, appropriated
from the German soldier he captured in the fall of 1918,
can be seen hanging from the back of his jacket.*

reorganization of exhibition themes at the Smithsonian. Stubby, after languishing for decades kenneled in a packing crate on an archival storage shelf, spent several years on exhibition at the state armory in Hartford. Conroy's grandson answered newspaper queries about the famous mascot, too, and he was the first family member I found when I began tracking the scattered trail of evidence that his grandfather had left behind.

In 2004, Stubby returned to a place of honor at the Smithsonian Institution. He is one of 16 key artifacts displayed in the World War I section of the "Price of Freedom" gallery, a comprehensive overview of American warfare that is one of the featured permanent exhibitions at the National Museum of American History. There Stubby stands, behind protective glass, in profile, his head ever cocked to the right, eyes focused on the horizon. A gas-mask-wearing doughboy towers over him clutching a bayonet-tipped rifle. Cher Ami, bless the poor bird's heart, stands beside him, perpetually balanced on its one remaining leg.

Stubby's jacket is not on display. The weight of all those medals pulling on the thin chamois leather would, given enough time, tear the material, so it resides in a customized archival storage box, as does Stubby's harness and other assorted memorabilia. The mascot's scrapbook, so legitimately dog-eared at this point that it has come apart from its binding, has now been digitally scanned as an added measure of preservation.

The day after we opened the Conroy history box, Alex, Curt, and their brother Jon and I visited Stubby at the Smithsonian. Four of Conroy's great-granddaughters joined us. Smithsonian curator Kathy Golden graciously opened up a conference room for the party and filled it with Stubby's belongings. For two hours, family members passed around the Mylar-protected pages of the scrapbook, laughing at lines here, commenting on family resemblances there, marveling at the dog's fame and their patriarch's devotion to him. Then we visited Stubby, himself, at the "Price of Freedom" hall, and family members posed in front of the mascot's case. If Conroy could have been there, he would have been beaming. I beamed in his place.

Robert Conroy and his friends from the Great War knew something that took decades for the U.S. military to figure out: Dogs and soldiers go together. Today we take it for granted that military service dogs help soldiers find hidden explosive devices, that they are essential team members on Navy Seal raids such as the one that stormed the residence of Osama bin Laden, and that they can still add their teeth to the fight, just the way Stubby did in 1919. Today we are even learning, as David E. Sharpe has shown through Companions For Heroes, that dogs have remarkable powers for healing old wounds, for restoring a sense of purpose in the wake of unspeakable trauma, for making a person feel whole once more. The shell-shocked veterans of World War I could have used such dogs. Robert Conroy was lucky enough to have one.

The U.S. military made official use of dogs during the Second World War. Among other duties, they served as sentries, delivered messages, scouted combat zones, listened for enemy aircraft, and helped recover the dead. Hundreds of dogs traveled to Asia during the Vietnam War, making such an impact on the troops that some fans advocated (unsuccessfully) for the addition of a military service dog to the sculptures at the Vietnam Veterans Memorial in Washington, D.C. As far back as the First World War, veterans had sought to recognize their four-footed companions. Who could forget those rescue dogs that had combed the battlefields with medicine, bandages, and water? In that case a memorial did become a reality; it stands in the nation's oldest pet cemetery, north of New York City in Hartsdale, New York.

Those soldiers from a century ago could not have imagined all the roles dogs would go on to play in the military, but they probably wouldn't be surprised by the services they now render, on battlefields and beyond. Dogs serve in the police force. They use their sense of smell to unearth everything from illegal drugs to missing persons to the scat that helps scientists study endangered species. They patrol golf courses to keep them free from destructive flocks of geese. They work hard—like dogs—because that's what they like to do. Scientists are beginning to better understand why: Dogs complete people like no other animal can, and vice versa. Connections forged 12,000 or more years ago, when wolves and domesticated dogs diverged, happened for a reason. Humans and dogs both benefited from the alliance. And they still do.

In 1918, after the fighting stopped, and even eight years later when Stubby died, Americans thought the memory of the Great War would last forever. "Down through the coming ages, into time not yet reckoned, there will be stories and tales of valor unfolded; vivid descriptions of the beginning of the drive at Château-Thierry, the smashing of the Hindenburg Line, the closing of the St. Mihiel salient or the bloody drive through the Argonne Forest." So wrote a contributor to the *New Britain Herald* on the occasion of Stubby's death in 1926. "All these will form traditions ranking with the best with which this country has ever been bound," the writer assured the paper's readers.

The tribute continued: "But, to New England folks, whose sons were members of the Yankee Division, 'New England's Own,' there will be one story which will ever be dear to those whose memory still holds the picture of the dark days of 1917-18 when the youth of this nation was striving to uphold the country's glorious record on the field of battle. That story will be the history of Stubby, the mascot of the 102nd Regiment, 26th Division."

At least some of these lofty predictions have come true. Details of battles may have dimmed, but the tale of Stubby's life *has* come down through the years of history. His story endures as testimony to the love that grows, even in the darkest days of combat; to the trust that means true friendship; to the devotion that one man can show for a dog—a devotion so strong that, decades after the man's death and almost a century after the birth of their friendship, their story not only endures, it thrives. It thrives and inspires, just as that journalist had long-ago forecast, just as Robert Conroy had always hoped it would, as one of the great stories to come down through the ages.

The story of a man and his dog, a dog and his man, inseparably bonded for life and ever after.

RESEARCH NOTES
AND
ACKNOWLEDGMENTS

T HE STORY OF THE CREATION OF *SERGEANT STUBBY* IS THE
story of its acknowledgments. For starters, there would
be no book were it not for J. Robert Conroy. His devotion to his friend, even after Stubby's death, accounts for the exis-
tence of this book. Had Conroy not succeeded in placing Stubby
in the Smithsonian, the dog's fame would surely have faded and
been lost. By making the Smithsonian the central repository for
all things Stubby, including the dog's scrapbook, he assured that
a core collection of archival materials would endure into the ages.
Thank you, Bob Conroy!

Of all the surviving artifacts, Stubby included, it is his scrapbook that best preserves his story. It serves as a cipher for understanding the old mascot's historical pedigree. Conroy created the
book with love, not with the training of a historian, so the album
has its drawbacks. Most of the articles Conroy saved were clipped
without evidence of publication date or place. The process of
identifying the provenance for these stories was a tedious one. I
was able to trace many of them through online databases for such
newspapers as the *New York Times,* the *Washington Post,* and
the *Hartford Courant.* Incredibly helpful Connecticut librarians
(more on these women later) helped pinpoint others. Some articles

continue to float unattributed, but even they begin to fall into place using the context of their content.

I made three trips to the National Museum of American History over the course of three years so that I could study Stubby's scrapbook, and that research forms the core of this book's content. Fortunately Smithsonian staffers have now made high-resolution scans of this artifact's content. Nearly 100 years old, the scrapbook's pages are no longer bound together (or in order, in my opinion), and its clippings have become aged and brittle. The scans will make it easier and safer for curators to share the album with Stubby's fans.

I am particularly grateful to Kathy Golden, associate curator for the Smithsonian's Division of Armed Forces History. Kathy is Stubby's keeper, and she guards her charge with critical devotion. Having become convinced that I was serious about my pursuit of his story, she could not have been more gracious, supportive, or helpful to my work. I am particularly grateful for the arrangements she made that allowed Conroy's descendants and me to spend a morning with her and Stubby's archival material. Kathy's colleague Kay Peterson, at the Archives Center for the National Museum of American History, hosted my other two visits with the scrapbook. She handles the digital files of the album, too, and provided the artwork for its reproductions in this book.

Connecticut librarians played an important role during my research. Pat Watson, head of adult services for the New Britain Public Library, provided an early cache of articles about Stubby that introduced me to previously unseen material. Later on I was able to visit in person with Pat and her colleague Oneil Cormier and conduct additional research on-site. Of particular help was the library's collection of city directories. These pre-phone address books helped to confirm the living and working history of Conroy and his family members.

The best article in Stubby's scrapbook, in my opinion, is one that lost its provenance on its way to preservation. "Three Canine War Heroes Enjoying Peace in Connecticut After Thrilling Trials Under Fire Along Western Front," reads its title, but there are no clues as to where it was originally published. This feature-length profile of Stubby and fellow war dog veterans Tuck and Toute de Suite offers some of the only surviving quotes by Conroy about his companion. It is one of the few articles from Stubby's lifetime to bear a byline, and its author, Bab Vickrey, offers firsthand accounts of Stubby's personality and behavior. The article is so large that it never fit properly in the scrapbook. Over time, the overhanging edge of the clipping began to erode, and now the article literally breaks off at the point where the author describes Stubby's behavior when he is petted.

Librarians, though, are not easily defeated by mysteries or dead ends. The scrapbook clipping did, at least, preserve a publication date, and my initial guess was that the story had appeared in Conroy's own *New Britain Herald*. When that hunch proved incorrect, local librarian Pat Watson was able to identify the author as someone who had written for the *Bridgeport Herald*. Enter another wonderful Connecticut librarian, Mary Witkowski. She and her colleague Robert Jeffries traced the story to their local newspaper and provided me with an intact copy of the article.

My biggest break in the researching of this animal love story came thanks to one of those newspaper articles provided by Pat Watson. This clipping led me to Curtis Deane, Conroy's eldest grandson. Curt became the living link to the past who helped me complete this book. Without Curt, Stubby's trail essentially died with his passing in 1926. A couple of stray clippings gave hints of what followed—the loss and rediscovery of Stubby's portrait, Conroy's escape in 1954 from that D.C. fire—but Conroy had kept himself so much in the background during

Stubby's lifetime that he essentially vanished from the record after his friend's death.

Curt helped to fill that gap, literally working in parallel to my efforts, tracking down birth certificates, digging out family records, introducing me to family members, and more. Curt knew about his grandfather's association with the Bureau of Investigation, now the FBI, and he placed the Freedom of Information Act request that yielded his grandfather's personnel file. The unearthing of this document served as another of the transformative moments during my research journey. When required to tell about himself, Conroy quite plainly stated his education and work history on FBI applications. Details previously unknown or only hinted at in newspaper clippings now could be placed within a coherent framework. Without this personnel file, Conroy would remain very much in the shadows in this book.

Research for a book is based on a combination of good luck and strategic, logical legwork. I wanted to write a book about Stubby, so it made sense to visit the Smithsonian. I wanted to write about World War I, so I toured the World War I Museum in Kansas City, Missouri—the nation's only center devoted exclusively to this conflict.

And so it went. Conroy had grown up in New Britain, Connecticut; I traveled to see it. Conroy had trained and met Stubby on the Yale athletic fields; I toured the grounds of the Yale Bowl and walked the turf of the playing fields. I combed through the university's archives for evidence of war-era activity, and I searched in vain for proof that Conroy had attended Yale, as his descendants thought (a mystery later solved by the FBI file's clarification that he had audited his Yale classes, thus leaving him omitted from official rolls).

Conroy had served in the 26th Division, so I combed through related archives at the Army War College Institute for Military

History in Carlisle, Pennsylvania. The Connecticut State Library, the West Haven Veterans Museum and Learning Center (home to Stubby's portrait and other artifacts from the 102nd Regiment), Georgetown University, the homes of Conroy's descendants— every stop helped.

Even such strategic study inevitably yields unexpected dividends. At Yale, for example, I found a treasure trove of period photographs from the war era, and I became engrossed by the annotated autograph books that were donated to the university by Elizabeth Hudson, an American nurse at the American Red Cross hospital in Neuilly, Paris. Likewise, at the Army War College Institute for Military History I encountered photographs by the archival-boxful that documented the life of the 26th Division. Such images not only become the illustrations for books like this one, they serve as incredibly rich primary source evidence of what soldiers did, how the military worked, and what things looked like in an earlier period—from equipment to dress to living conditions and more. Researchers such as I are forever indebted to the eyewitnesses who recorded such scenes and to the librarians and archivists who curate the past so that it stays alive.

Many others contributed to this book through email correspondence or phone calls. Mary Thurston, historian for the nation's oldest pet cemetery in Hartsdale, New York, astutely pointed out the consistency with which Stubby's photographs show him with flattened ears. Staffers at the National Guard Archives in Concord, Massachusetts, combed their records for evidence of Conroy's outbound passage to Europe. John Fox, FBI historian, clarified a point of photo research for me. Jean Shulman provided details about the American Red Cross records related to Stubby. Everett G. Shepherd of the Connecticut American Legion introduced me to the state's incredibly helpful *Service Records,* an annotated listing of all World War I service members from the Nutmeg State.

Every writer of nonfiction knows that research can go on forever but that deadlines require a pivot from gatherer to sharer. In Stubby's case, I had the remarkable good fortune to be able to share this history not once, but twice. First I wrote about him for young people—*Stubby the War Dog: The True Story of World War I's Bravest Dog*—a heavily illustrated history published by the children's book division of the National Geographic Society simultaneously with the release of this accounting for adults. Turning from the first account to the second could have been a writer's nightmare version of *Groundhog Day*. Thankfully it was not. I followed the writing of the first book with additional research, and I approached the adult book as a fresh assignment.

I've spent almost two decades writing for young people, and the opportunity to write for adults proved to be more liberating than I'd imagined and less terrifying than I'd feared. After the work began, I found myself luxuriating in longer sentences and my natural vocabulary, freed from having to artfully weave in the contexts that adults take for granted. (Think, what is a bayonet? Or why didn't they just use their cell phones? Or what was vaudeville?)

The team at the National Geographic Society could not have been more supportive. My colleagues in the children's book division have equally wonderful counterparts working with adult books, starting with my editor, Bridget English. She believed in this story from the moment she heard of it. Her confidence and careful tending empowered and enabled me to bring it to life. I appreciate the transformative support of Janet Goldstein, editorial director of the adult book division; Susan Blair, director of photography for adult books, and her colleague Galen Young; Melissa Farris, who deserves a hearty cheer for her design of this book's wonderful cover; as well as Katie Olsen for executing its interior layout. Many thanks to one and all.

Historians Edward G. Lengel and Michael E. Shay deserve double thanks. For starters, they each wrote masterly and invaluable histories of World War I—Lengel's *To Conquer Hell* and Shay's *The Yankee Division in the First World War*—which provided me with invaluable background information about the scene that Stubby and Conroy entered in 1917. Furthermore, each of these scholars thoughtfully reviewed my book in manuscript form, helping me clarify several points in the historical record. Curtis Deane likewise reviewed the manuscript for me and patiently answered my many queries, each of us determined to do the historical record proud.

Then, of course, there are the friends and family who stand behind any author's creations. My parents, Henry and Dolores, inspire me with their good humor, creativity, and fortitude, even as they push toward and into their 90s. My 20-something sons, Sam and Jake, are the reasons I write. My brother, David, and his wife, Mary, are priceless friends as well as remarkable allies—at the ready with paintbrushes, for example, after I bought a new home, so that I could get back to Stubby that much faster and amidst cheery surroundings.

Writing friends include children's book authors Jamie Swenson, who offered invaluable insights during her review of this manuscript, as well as Georgia Beaverson, Pam Beres, Karen Blumenthal, Judy Bryan, Elizabeth Fixmer, and Sue Macy. Personal friends, including Hester, Kedron, Marty, Peggy, and Shawn, watch me drop from sight—off on another research trail or hounded by deadlines—and wait patiently while I disappear, making the resurfacing that much sweeter.

Curtis Deane and his family have become friends and allies during the making of these books, one of those unexpected bits of lagniappe that comes from my line of work. And then, of course, I must thank Stubby himself—for being such a wonderful subject to explore, for reminding me how it felt, many years ago, to adore a dog, and for making it possible for me to imagine doing so again. What a gift!

APPENDIX

Stubby's Uniform
An Annotated List of Medals and Decorations

Compiled by Ann Bausum, with the assistance of Kathy Golden, Associate Curator, Division of Armed Forces History, National Museum of American History, Smithsonian Institution.

Left flank, head to tail (14 items).

- Top, three-bar service stripe (equals 18 months of service)
- Middle, red honorable discharge stripe
- Bottom, 26th Yankee Division patch
- Top, Verdun medal (red ribbon with pencil stripes of white and blue)
- Bottom, General Service Button 25-ligne (1 of 4)
- American Legion badge from Minneapolis (red, white, and blue ribbon)
- New Haven World War I veterans medal

  Text, reverse side: To her sons who went forth to war that their homes might remain at peace 1917–1919
- France, commemorative medal for WWI (red and white striped ribbon)

  Text, reverse side: République Française Grand Guerre 1914–1918
- Top, "Lindsay" Canadian maple leaf
- Bottom left, St. Mihiel medal (gold-red-gold ribbon)

Stubby's military uniform rests protectively flattened in an archival storage box at the Smithsonian's National Museum of American History. His wound stripe appears on the jacket's right flank; his three service chevrons appear on the left, next to the decorative braid that spells his name.

- Bottom right, General Service Button 25-ligne (2 of 4)
- Purple Heart
- Château-Thierry medal (white ribbon)
- American Legion medal, from St. Paul, Minnesota, 5th/6th (faded ribbon)

Right flank, tail to head (18 items):
- "Foreign Service / American Red Cross" medal (blue and white ribbon)
- Upper, General Service Button 25-ligne (3 of 4)
- Lower, American Legion badge, from New Orleans (blue ribbon)

  Text: engraved, Guest, 4th Annual Convention, New Orleans, American Legion; hand-printed, STUBBY
- Top, Maréchal Foch medal
- Middle, Chatillon (filigree medal with palm leaf design)
- Bottom, American Legion badge, 3rd convention, Kansas City (dark striped ribbon)

  Text: engraved, Kansas City; typed, guest Stubby AEF Mascot
- Top left, Jeanne d'Arc medal

  Text: Jeanne 1412-1431 d'Arc
- Top right, crest from Brest, France
- Middle left, blue cross of Lorraine, perhaps emblem of 79th Infantry Division
- Middle right, Ste. Genevieve pin
- Bottom left, General Service Button 25-ligne (3 of 4)
- Bottom right, American Legion badge, tan and striped ribbon, Omaha

  Text: engraved, 7th Annual Convention, Omaha, 1925; hand-printed, Stubby
- Top, Verdun medal, text on reverse: 21 Fevier 1916

  Note: duplicate of Verdun medal on other flank of jacket, but this one has no ribbon or clasp.

213

- Bottom, U.S. World War I Victory Medal with five battle clasps (denoting battlefield service):
    - Champagne-Marne
    - Aisne-Marne
    - St. Mihiel
    - Meuse-Argonne
    - Defensive Sector
- Humane Education Society medal

  Text: Stubby May 13, 1921; this is the medal awarded by General Pershing
- Top, wound stripe
- Bottom, 26th Yankee Division patch
- Far right, VFW badge, for Stubby (red, white, and blue ribbon)

General adornment (3 items):
- Center, back, Victory patch (embroidered wreath–flags of Allies)
- Center, front, overcoat button that holds the coat together with 35-ligne general service button
- Left flank, partly covered by medals, "Stubby 102nd US INF" braid sewn to fabric

TIME LINE

1892
• James Joseph Conroy, later known as J. Robert Conroy, is born on February 27 in New Britain, Connecticut, the third of six children.

1899
• James P. Conroy, father of J. Robert Conroy, dies on September 25 in New Britain, Connecticut.

1912
• Woodrow Wilson is elected the 28th President of the United States. He is sworn in on March 4, 1913.

1913
• Alice McAvay Conroy, mother of J. Robert Conroy, dies on March 15 in New Britain, Connecticut.

1914
• The assassination of Archduke Francis Ferdinand on June 28 sets off events that lead to World War I. The German invasion of Belgium on August 4 marks the beginning of combat. President Wilson declares U.S. neutrality in the conflict.

1915
• The sinking of the *Lusitania* on May 7 elevates the tensions between the United States and Germany.

1916
• Woodrow Wilson wins reelection with the campaign slogan, "He kept us out of war." His Second Inaugural ceremony occurs on March 5, 1917.

215

1917

• On February 1, Kaiser Wilhelm II announces that his nation will soon resume submarine attacks on nonwarring ships bound for Allied ports. The surfacing of the so-called Zimmerman telegram later that month increases the likelihood that the United States will join the war.

• On April 6, the United States declares war on Germany and prepares to enter the fight.

• Conroy enlists in the Connecticut National Guard on May 21, the first step toward joining the U.S. Army. Soon after, he begins his military training on the athletic fields of Yale University in New Haven, Connecticut.

• On June 14, Maj. Gen. John J. Pershing and his team of advisers settle in France so they can plan for the arrival of American forces later in the year.

• A stray dog befriends Conroy and other service members during the summer at their training ground in Connecticut. They name him Stubby, and he begins to live alongside them and shadow their routines.

• Conroy's National Guard unit becomes a part of the 26th or Yankee Division of the U.S. Army; Conroy departs Connecticut with members of the 102nd Infantry in September, bound for Newport News, Virginia. Stubby tags along.

• When Conroy's unit heads to Europe aboard the *Minnesota,* Conroy arranges for Stubby to be smuggled aboard. They reach France in early October and head inland for further training.

1918

• Conroy and Stubby reach the front lines of France on February 5 to help defend battle lines along the Chemin des Dames highway. Stubby experiences his first gas attack there in late March.

• On April 5, Conroy receives his first military promotion, to private 1st class.

• In early April, the Yankee Division begins defending territory near Toul, France. Several weeks later, on April 20, Stubby is seriously wounded by shrapnel during what becomes known as the battle of Seicheprey. He spends six weeks in a military hospital recovering from his injuries before rejoining Conroy and his unit.

• During the summer, Conroy and Stubby take part in defensive, and then offensive, campaigns along the Marne River, including the liberation of Château-Thierry in late July. Grateful women from that city make Stubby a uniform.

• Conroy and Stubby participate in the St. Mihiel campaign starting on September 12. The 26th Division retakes the desired territory from the Germans in four days.

• Allied forces begin the Meuse-Argonne campaign on September 26, an undertaking designed to defeat the German forces and end the war. It lasts for weeks with varying degrees of intensity along multiple points at the front lines. The Yankee Division, including Conroy and Stubby, take part in a diversionary operation when the campaign begins; Stubby captures a German soldier during this maneuver.

• Conroy receives his second and final military promotion, to corporal, on September 30.

• On November 2, Conroy is "wounded in action slightly" by poison gas when the Germans attack the Bois d'Ormont north of Verdun during the Meuse-Argonne campaign. Stubby is likewise injured. Both Conroy and Stubby make a full recovery following a brief hospitalization and return together to the battlefront.

• The warring nations sign an armistice agreement, and all combat ceases on November 11 at 11 o'clock in the morning.

• Later that fall, the Yankee Division settles into its winter quarters at Montigny-le-Roi, France, awaiting its return to the United States.

• President Woodrow Wilson spends Christmas Day, December 25, with the Yankee Division. Stubby reportedly shakes hands with the President during his visit.

1919

• On March 13, Conroy and Stubby begin a two-week furlough, intending to visit the south of France, but Conroy becomes ill with influenza and requires hospitalization in Paris. Stubby receives permission to stay with him. Conroy is discharged in time for the pair to visit Monte Carlo before their furlough ends on March 27.

• Conroy and Stubby depart from Brest, France, on March 31, sailing on the *Agamemnon* with other members of the 102nd Regiment and the Yankee Division. They reach Boston Harbor on April 7.

• Stubby leads the 102nd Regiment in the Boston victory parade on April 25, celebrating the return of the Yankee Division.

• On April 26, Conroy receives an honorable discharge from the U.S. military. He and Stubby depart for visits and celebrations in various Connecticut cities.

• Stubby begins a three-day engagement on May 1 at the Bijou Theatre in New Haven, Connecticut, appearing with Conroy as part of a vaudeville show of live performances and other entertainment.

• On May 8, Stubby receives a lifetime membership in the YMCA, good for "three bones a day" and "a place to sleep."

• Representatives sign the Treaty of Versailles on June 28, marking the official end of World War I; however, the U.S. Senate subsequently rejects the agreement, and a separate treaty is negotiated later on. It is signed and ratified in 1921.

• Stubby accompanies Conroy to the first convention of the newly formed American Legion when the veterans' organization meets in Minneapolis, Minnesota, November 10–12.

1920
• Stubby receives a Hero Dog Award in February at the Eastern Dog Club show in Boston. Later that spring the group awards him a silver medallion and ceremonial harness.

• That fall Conroy moves with Stubby to Washington, D.C., and enrolls in the law school at Catholic University. Stubby becomes the mascot for the university's football team. In 1921, he becomes the mascot for the Georgetown University Hilltoppers (later known as the Hoyas) after Conroy switches to that university's law school.

1921

• Stubby is awarded a "special prize" from the Boston Terrier Club in Washington, D.C., on March 7.

• Stubby is one of the featured participants in a mid-May animal parade in Washington, D.C., organized by the Humane Education Society, an animal rights group.

• Stubby and Conroy attend a party for wounded veterans, held on the grounds of the White House on June 8. They meet President Warren G. Harding and First Lady Florence Harding during the event.

• On July 6, General Pershing presents Stubby with a medal from the Humane Education Society to celebrate his work as a rescue dog during World War I and to commemorate his participation in the society's recent animal parade.

• Conroy and Stubby join other veterans during October for an American Legion convention in Kansas City, Missouri. Military leaders from the Allied forces gather with veterans to dedicate the site where the Liberty Memorial will be built, commemorating the Great War. In subsequent years Conroy and Stubby take part in American Legion conventions in New Orleans (1922), St. Paul (1924), and Omaha (1925).

1923

• Conroy interrupts his law studies to join the Bureau of Investigation at the Justice Department, forerunner of the FBI. He begins his service in July and resigns 16 months later on October 11, 1924.

1924

• Congress passes the World War Adjusted Compensation Act, known as the Bonus Act, offering Great War veterans deferred compensation for their military service, payable in 1945.

• On October 29, Conroy and Stubby are invited to visit the White House to meet with President Calvin Coolidge.

1925

• Conroy begins working on Capitol Hill, serving as secretary for Congressman Edward Hart Fenn, Republican from Connecticut. Later he serves as clerk for the Committee on the Census, chaired by Fenn.

• Charles Ayer Whipple, the artist for the U.S. Capitol, paints a portrait of Stubby wearing his jacket and military honors.

• Conroy and Stubby attend their final American Legion convention together when they travel to Omaha, Nebraska, during October.

1926

• Stubby dies at home, cradled in Conroy's arms, on March 16. Conroy immediately makes arrangements to have the mascot's remains preserved.

• Conroy graduates from law school on June 12, having completed his studies at National University. He gains admission to the bar of the Supreme Court of the District of Columbia on October 11, 1927.

1927

• Conroy marries Ruth M. Burghardt on June 4. They separate about seven months later. Their daughter, Elaine Virginia Conroy, is born on July 20, 1928, in Washington, D.C.

• On December 7, Stubby's remains go on exhibition at the headquarters of the American Red Cross, on long-term loan from Conroy.

1932

• Depression-era veterans in need of funds organize a Bonus Expeditionary Force that descends on Washington, D.C., seeking early payment of their World War I service bonuses. After weeks of encampment, the protesters are routed from the city and dispersed, only to return in subsequent years until their demands are met in 1936.

1941

• The United States joins the Second World War (which began in 1939), following the bombing of Pearl Harbor, Hawaii, by the Japanese on December 7. Conroy registers for military service in 1942 and reportedly works stateside on military intelligence.

1954

• Conroy and Stubby make the news when Conroy flees a burning high-rise in Washington, D.C., on April 21, carrying the stuffed remains of Stubby under his arm.

1956
• On May 22, Conroy presents Stubby to the Smithsonian Institution along with the mascot's scrapbook, medal-bedecked jacket, collar, and ceremonial harness.

1975
• Conroy, who has retired to Florida, marries Margaret Elmyra Cooper on December 20 at age 83, his second marriage.

1987
• James Robert Conroy dies in West Palm Beach, Florida, on April 25 at the age of 95. His remains are cremated and laid to rest in that city.

2004
• Stubby goes on permanent display at the Smithsonian in the "Price of Freedom" exhibit at the National Museum of American History.

BIBLIOGRAPHY

"102d Mascot Made Life Member of Y.M.C.A." *Hartford Courant,* May 9, 1919, 12.

Benwell, Harry A. *History of the Yankee Division.* Boston: The Cornhill Company, 1919.

Berg, A. Scott. *Wilson.* New York: G. P. Putnam's Sons, 2013.

Berlin, Irving. "Over the Sea." New York: Waterson, Berlin & Snyder Co., 1918.

"Body of Stubby, 26th Division Dog, Will Be on View." *Hartford Courant,* August 21, 1926, 11.

Brands, H. W. *Woodrow Wilson,* The American Presidents. Arthur M. Schlesinger, Jr., gen. ed. New York: Times Books, Henry Holt and Company, 2003.

Brinkley, Alan and Davis Dyer, editors. *The Reader's Companion to the American Presidency.* Boston: Houghton Mifflin, 2004.

Capozzola, Christopher. *Uncle Sam Wants You: World War I and the Making of the Modern American Citizen.* New York: Oxford University Press, 2008.

Cohan, George M. "Over There." New York: Leo Feist, Inc., 1917.

"Col. J. H. Parker Commands 102d." *Hartford Courant,* February 20, 1918, 5.

"Connecticut at Kansas City." *New Britain Herald,* 1921, editorial.*

Conrad, Robert J. "Stubby's Legend Revived by Visit to State Armory," *Hartford Courant,* January 25, 1998.

Conroy, J. Robert. "Stubby A.E.F. Mascot." Scrapbook compiled and annotated by Conroy, held by Smithsonian Institution, National Museum of American History, Washington, D.C.

———. "Stubby, the Story of a Dog Who Made Himself Famous." Published in the *Communique*, the American Legion, Trenton Post 93, January 1967.

———. "'Stubby' Dog Mascot of Yankee Division Mourned by Soldiers." Obituary published 1926.*

"Crowds Throng to Dog Show." *Boston Traveler*, February 25, 1920.

Daly, John J. "Sergeant Major Jiggs." *Washington Post*, January 16, 1927, SM: 1.

Daniels, Roger. *Guarding the Golden Door: American Immigration Policy and Immigrants Since 1882*. New York: Hill and Wang, 2004.

Deane, Curtis. Interviews conducted by Ann Bausum, February 11, 2013; March 9, 2013; April 2, 2013; May 4, 2013; and subsequent correspondence.

DeGregorio, William A. *The Complete Book of U.S. Presidents*. New York: Wings Books, Random House, 2005 (sixth edition, revised).

Derr, Mark. *A Dog's History of America*. New York: North Point Press, 2004.

"A Dog of War." *Chicago Tribune*, October 30, 1921, 4.

"Dog Parade to Open 'Mutt' Show Today." *Washington Post*, November 20, 1925, 2.

"Dogs and the Soldier." *Our Dumb Animals*, newsletter for the Massachusetts Society for the Prevention of Cruelty to Animals (Norwood), Vol. 51, No. 6, November 1918.

"Edwards at Yankee Division Reunion." *New York Times*, July 4, 1921.

"Ex-Service Men United With Comrades Again at Christmas Dinner." *Hartford Courant*, December 26, 1922, 1, 2.

"The Faithful Dog." *Washington Post*, September 11, 1925, editorial: 6.

Fogle, Bruce. *Dog: The Definitive Guide for Dog Owners*. Buffalo, New York: Firefly Books, 2010.

Ford, Linda G. *Iron-Jawed Angels: The Suffrage Militancy of the National Woman's Party, 1912–1920.* Lanham, Maryland: University Press of America, 1991.

Franklin, Jon. *The Wolf in the Parlor: How the Dog Came to Share Your Brain.* New York: Henry Holt and Company, 2009.

"General Edwards at Reunion Today." *Hartford Courant,* August 28, 1920, 2.

"Gen. Edwards 'Idol of Outfit,' Says Conn. Governor." *Hartford Courant,* April 8, 1919, 6.

"General Pershing Decorates A.E.F. Dog Hero." *Army and Navy Journal,* undated.*

" 'Got Two Germans Before They Got Me'—Plumridge." *Hartford Courant,* August 20, 1918, 3.

"Greatest of War Dogs to Attend Big Game." *Washington Post,* November 1, 1924, S1.

" 'Happyland'—Even the Dog Wears the Smile That Means 'We're Home Again.' " *Boston American,* April 10, 1919, 3.

"Harding Applauds Animal Parade." *Washington Post,* May 14, 1921, 4.

Hare, Brian and Vanessa Woods. *The Genius of Dogs: How Dogs Are Smarter Than You Think.* New York: The Penguin Group, Dutton, 2013.

Hausman, Joshua K. "Fiscal Policy and Economic Recovery: The Case of the 1936 Veterans' Bonus." Unpublished paper, October 29, 2012, University of California, Berkeley. http://econgrads.berkeley.edu/jhausman/research/

"Here Are Three Fellow Warriors." *Sunday News* (Omaha, Nebraska), October 25, 1925.

"Hero Dog Hotel Guest." *New York Times,* December 31, 1922.

Irwin, Inez Hayes. *The Story of Alice Paul and the National Woman's Party.* Fairfax, Virginia: Denlinger's Publishers, 1964, 1977.

"James Conroy and His War Hero Dog in City." *Daily Press* (Newport News, Virginia), June 19, 1923, 9.

Janis, Elsie. *The Big Show: My Six Months with the American Expeditionary Forces.* New York: Cosmopolitan Book Corporation: 1919.

Kelley, Ralph J. "Stubby, the Canine Hero of the A.E.F." *Washington Post,* November 15, 1925, SM: 1, 5.

Kennedy, David M. *Over Here: The First World War and American Society.* New York: Oxford University Press, 2005.

Keyssar, Alexander. *The Right to Vote: The Contested History of Democracy in the United States.* New York: Basic Books, 2000.

Kinghorn, Jonathan. *The Atlantic Transport Line, 1881–1931.* Jefferson, North Carolina: McFarland and Company, Inc., 2012.

Knapp, Arthur L. "Coolidge May See Game with Gen. Calles of Mexico." *Washington Post,* November 1, 1924, S1.

"Last of Stubby, a Dog Hero." *New Britain Herald,* March 18, 1926, 6.

Lemish, Michael G. *War Dogs: A History of Loyalty and Heroism.* Washington, D.C.: Potomac Books, 2008.

Lengel, Edward G. *To Conquer Hell: The Meuse-Argonne, 1918, the Epic Battle That Ended the First World War.* New York: Henry Holt and Company, 2008.

" 'The Lucky Dog.' " *Boston Traveler,* April 26, 1919.

Manning, George H. "Fenn Presents 'Stubby' Plaque." *New Britain Herald,* December 7, 1927.

"Mascot of Army to Arrive Today." *Times-Picayune* (New Orleans), October 15, 1922.

"Mascots as Popular Today as They Were Centuries Ago." *New York Times,* April 17, 1927.

"Mascots Include Dog and a Goat." *Hartford Courant,* April 8, 1919, 1, 11.

Mickey, Lisa D. "Chasing Off Wildlife, With Course Etiquette." *New York Times,* September 2, 2013, D7.

"Most Decorated Dog in A.E.F." *Jacksonville Courier* (Jacksonville, Illinois), May 19, 1921, 1.

Nicholson, Tim, and Philomena Rutherford. *The Reader's Digest Illustrated Book of Dogs, 2nd rev. ed.* Pleasantville, New York: Reader's Digest Association, Inc., 1993.

"Now a Y.M.C.A. Life Member." *Hartford Courant,* May 11, 1919, 10.

Orlean, Susan. *Rin Tin Tin: The Life and the Legend.* New York: Simon & Schuster, 2011.

Owens, David. "A War Hero Stands Out." *Hartford Courant,* February 9, 1998.

"Pershing Honors Dog Hero." *Evening Bulletin* (Philadelphia, Pennsylvania), July 7, 1921.

"Pershing Honors Dog Mascot of A.E.F." *New York Times,* July 7, 1921, 1.

Photographic Supplement to Historical Record of Quartermaster Corps Activities A.E.F., Combat Troops at the Front. Tech. Rept. No. 2843-V8. Library of Congress, Prints and Photographs Collection, LOT 8330.

"Portrait of Stubby, Dog War Hero, Found." *New York Times,* January 18, 1931.

Preston, Diana. Lusitania: *An Epic Tragedy.* New York: Berkley Books, 2003.

"Report of General John J. Pershing, U.S.A." Cabled to the Secretary of War, November 20, 1918; corrected January 16, 1919.

Richardson, Richard L. "A Crack at Stubby." *Stars and Stripes* (Washington, D.C.), August 27, 1921, letters to the editor, 5.

Rohan, Jack. *Rags: The Story of a Dog Who Went to War.* New York: Harper & Brothers Publishers, 1930.

Schmidt, Regin. *Red Scare: FBI and the Origins of Anticommunism in the United States, 1919–1943.* Copenhagen, Denmark: University of Copenhagen, Museum Tusculanum Press, 2000.

"Seicheprey Anniversary on Saturday." *Hartford Courant,* April 16, 1928, 14.

"Seicheprey YD War Hero." Connecticut Department, Veterans of Foreign Wars, April 1926.

"Semper Fido." *Washington Post,* November 14, 1993, Style: F1, F4, F5.

Service Records, Connecticut: Men and Women in the Armed Forces of the United States During World War, 1917–1920. Vols. 1, 2 & 3. Hartford, Connecticut: Office of the Adjutant General, State Armory, publication undated.

Shay, Michael E. *Revered Commander, Maligned General: The Life of Clarence Ransom Edwards, 1859–1931.* Columbia: University of Missouri Press, 2011.

———. *The Yankee Division in the First World War: In the Highest Tradition.* College Station: Texas A&M University Press, 2008.

Sibley, Frank P. *With the Yankee Division in France.* Boston: Little, Brown, and Company, 1919.

" 'Smiling Regiment,' Parker Calls 102d." *Hartford Courant,* March 12, 1918, 5.

Smith, Abbe. " 'Stubby' the Dog Recalled for WWI Heroism." *New Haven Register,* November 12, 2009.

"State Comes to Hartford to Take Soldier Sons to Her Arms Again." *Hartford Courant,* May 1, 1919, 1, 10, 11.

Stevens, Doris. *Jailed for Freedom.* New York: Boni and Liveright, 1920.

Stone, Geoffrey R. *Perilous Times: Free Speech in Wartime.* New York: W. W. Norton & Company, 2004.

"Stubby, 102d Mascot, Gets Third War Medal Decoration." *Hartford Courant,* July 8, 1921, 15.

" 'Stubby,' 102d Mascot, to Be Guest at Christmas Dinner." *Hartford Courant,* December 13, 1922, 24.

"Stubby Decorated for Heroism by Pershing." *Washington Star,* July 7, 1921.

" 'Stubby' Dies; Dog Gained Fame in War." *Washington Post,* March 17, 1926, 24.

" 'Stubby' Dog Hero in Parade Today." *Washington Post,* May 11, 1921, 16.

"Stubby, Dog Hero, Is Honored Again." *Washington Post,* July 7, 1921, 14.

" 'Stubby,' Famous War Dog, Becomes Full-Fledged Member of Eddy-Glover Post of American Legion." *New Britain Herald,* undated.*

"Stubby, Famous War Dog, Dies; Saw Action with 102d Regiment in France; Decorated by Pershing." *New Britain Herald,* March 17, 1926, 1, 15.

" 'Stubby' Has Hiked With His Pals on Every Legion Parade Route." *Minneapolis Morning Tribune,* September 17, 1924.

" 'Stubby,' Hero Dog, Is Awarded Medal at Show." *New Britain Herald,* February 24, 1920.

" 'Stubby,' Heroic Mascot of 102d Infantry, Dies in Washington Home." *Hartford Courant,* March 18, 1926, 2.

"Stubby's History of Epic Warfare." *New Britain Herald,* March 24, 1926.

" 'Stubby' Honored by General Pershing." *New Britain Herald,* July 7, 1921.

"Stubby, Legion Mascot, Here." *Kansas City Star,* October 1921.*

" 'Stubby,' Most Decorated Dog, Meets Buddies in Omaha." *Evening Bee* (Omaha, Nebraska), October 8, 1925.

"Stubby of the A.E.F. Enters Valhalla." *New York Times,* April 4, 1926.

" 'Stubby,' of the Yankee Division." *Hartford Courant,* April 13, 1919, 19.

"Stubby, War Dog Hero, Will Be C.U. Mascot in State Game." *Washington Post,* November 1, 1920, 12.

" 'Stubby,' War Mascot, Honored by Comrades." *Washington Post,* December 5, 1927, 2.

" 'Stubby' Will Have Tablet to Memory." *Hartford Courant,* November 30, 1927, 6.

" 'Stubby,' Yankee Division Mascot, Returns to Honor Human Buddies." *New Britain Herald,* December 26, 1922.

" 'Stubby,' YD Canine Hero, Dead." *New Haven Journal Courier,* 1926.

" 'Stubby,' YD Mascot, Wins More Honors." *Hartford Courant,* February 25, 1920, 4.

Swager, Peggy. *Boston Terrier.* Freehold, New Jersey: Kennel Club Books, Inc., 2011.

"Tablet Commemorating Deeds of Stubby Given to Red Cross by Fenn." *Hartford Courant,* December 8, 1927, 9.

"Tells of Regard for Gen. Edwards." *Hartford Courant,* March 14, 1919.

Thompson, John A. *Woodrow Wilson.* London, England: Pearson Education Limited, 2002.

Tucker, Ray T. "Ovation Without Parallel for New England's Own in Boston; 102d Wins Honors of Parade." *Hartford Courant,* April 26, 1919, 1, 2.

"Veterans of Yankee Division Will Meet." *Washington Post,* December 14, 1924, 27.

Vickrey, Bab. "Three Canine War Heroes Enjoying Peace in Connecticut After Thrilling Trials Under Fire Along Western Front." *Bridgeport Herald,* August 8, 1920.

Whitehead, Sarah. *Dog: The Complete Guide.* New York: Barnes and Noble Books, 1999.

"Works for a Bonus (and a Bone)." *New York American,* June 5, 1923, 9.

"Wounded Dog Calls on Former Buddies." *Middleton Evening Press,* July 23, 1921, 10.

Wyatt, Franklin P. "A Known Warrior." (Unidentified source), 1921, letters to the editor.*

"YD Dog Given Medal." *Boston Traveler,* July 7, 1921.

Zimmer, Carl. "Wolf to Dog, an Enduring Mystery." *New York Times,* November 19, 2013, D3.

* Publication information for some material taken from J. Robert Conroy's scrapbook for Stubby could not be confirmed.

ILLUSTRATIONS
CREDITS

Front cover: (Image of Stubby) Library of Congress Prints & Photographs Division, LC-DIG-hec-31070 (colorized by Melissa Farris); (background flag) Ensup/iStockphoto; 15, Bettmann/Corbis; 18-19, Library of Congress Prints & Photographs Division, PAN US MILITARY–Army no. 115; 26, Courtesy of the Deane family; 29, Courtesy of the U.S. Army Heritage and Education Center; 37, Courtesy of the U.S. Army Heritage and Education Center; 41, Elizabeth Hudson Papers, Manuscripts and Archives, Yale University Library; 47, Courtesy Armed Forces History, Smithsonian Institution; 50, Courtesy of the U.S. Army Heritage and Education Center; 56, Courtesy of the U.S. Army Heritage and Education Center; 63, Courtesy of the U.S. Army Heritage and Education Center; 70, Courtesy of the U.S. Army Heritage and Education Center; 74, Courtesy Armed Forces History, Smithsonian Institution; 81, Courtesy Armed Forces History, Smithsonian Institution; 89, Library of Congress Prints & Photographs Division, LC-DIG-ds-04292; 92-93, Library of Congress Prints & Photographs Division, LOT 6944 no. 32; 100, Library of Congress Prints & Photographs Division, LC-USZ62-51348; 103, Courtesy of the Sewall-Belmont House & Museum, Home of the Historic National Woman's Party; 110, Library of Congress Prints & Photographs Division, LC-USZ62-36565; 115, Courtesy of the U.S. Army Heritage and Education Center; 120, Courtesy of the U.S. Army Heritage and Education Center; 128, Paul Jean Gaston Darrot Papers, Manuscripts and Archives, Yale University Library; 133, Courtesy Armed Forces History, Smithsonian Institution; 138, Courtesy of the U.S. Army Heritage and Education Center; 140-141, Library of Congress Prints & Photographs Division, LC-USZ62-52796; 147, Courtesy Armed Forces History, Smithsonian Institution; 151, Courtesy Armed Forces History, Smithsonian Institution; 154, Courtesy Armed Forces History, Smithsonian Institution; 160-161, Courtesy Armed Forces History, Smithsonian Institution; 165, Bettmann/Corbis; 168, Courtesy Armed Forces History, Smithsonian Institution; 173, Library of Congress Prints & Photographs Division, LC-DIG-npcc-13409; 176, Courtesy of the Deane family; 181, Courtesy Armed Forces History, Smithsonian Institution; 184, Courtesy Armed Forces History, Smithsonian Institution; 191, Author's collection/Artifact from Armed Forces History, Smithsonian Institution; 199, Courtesy of the Deane family; 212, Author's collection/Artifact from Armed Forces History, Smithsonian Institution; Back cover, Courtesy Armed Forces History, Smithsonian Institution.

INDEX

READING GUIDE

1. Most Americans wanted the United States to stay out of the First World War. What reasons would the average American citizen most likely have given for neutrality?

2. The sinking of the *Lusitania* and other ships bearing American citizens and cargo influenced President Woodrow Wilson to involve the United States in the war. Why would Germany have considered it justifiable for civilians to perish during military attacks at sea?

3. British lieutenant Ralph Kynoch said, "We'll take anything for a trench companion—but give us a dog first" (page 43). What made dogs ideally suited to be companions to soldiers in the trenches? Were there risks in allowing members of the armed forces to keep dogs on the battlefield?

4. What factors motivated Stubby's companion, Robert Conroy, to smuggle his friend overseas? To what extent was he naive or insensitive to transport a dog to a war zone? What alternatives could he have considered, in terms of leaving the dog behind?

5. Like the soldiers of the Yankee Division, Stubby must have experienced unimaginable fear and uncertainty on the battlefield, but unlike the soldiers who befriended him, he could have more easily deserted the scene. What options might he have had beyond the battle zone? What factors influenced him to remain on the front lines instead?

6. Stubby seemed to have a knack for knowing when soldiers needed companionship or consolation in wartime (page 67). What cues would the men have given Stubby that allowed him

to recognize those needs? Soldiers may have thanked the dog for his companionship by sharing food with him. How else may he have been rewarded for offering his attention?

7. Robert Conroy wrote that Stubby "seemed to have many lives" (page 79), and there are conflicting reports about the quality of Stubby's bravery in the face of danger. As with most stories, the truth may have been changed or exaggerated with each telling. What value did these embellishments have to the community of soldiers that adopted Stubby as their mascot? What harm could the unvarnished truth have presented?

8. Communication between commanders and battle units is a critical factor in success on the battlefield. What challenges were presented in a war zone, where trenches restricted one's vision and communications were carried by fragile wiring or by human or animal messengers?

9. Civilians on the home front were asked to make sacrifices such as observing "meatless Mondays" and "wheatless Wednesdays" (page 99) to be sure there were enough resources to support the troops. Do you think Americans could be called on to make the same sacrifices today? What changes in American culture have influenced our ability or willingness to do these things in the 21st century? What types of home-front support do we provide our troops today?

10. What were the risks of a propaganda campaign that vilified Germany and the German war machine, tainting, by association, German Americans and German culture in the United States? Could the benefits have outweighed the harm to any extent? What long-term damage could this campaign have had on American culture?

11. Was it right for the National Woman's Party to pursue its goal of woman suffrage during wartime when many voices advocated for the country to stand united against a common foe? How might the timing of its efforts have contributed to the success of the movement and the ratification of the 19th Amendment, granting women the right to vote not even two years after the end of combat?

12. Historian Edward G. Lengel characterizes the Meuse-Argonne campaign as the largest and most costly battle in American

history, and he considers it to be America's most important contribution to the outcome of the First World War (page 125). Why has this campaign largely been forgotten?

13. The military euthanized thousands of service dogs after the war, considering them to be too traumatized by combat for repatriation (page 136). What fears or concerns might have prompted such a decision?

14. If it's easy to understand why soldiers embraced Stubby as a mascot on the battlefield, it may be more difficult to comprehend why civilians were so eager to celebrate him after the war. What would he and his story have represented for everyday Americans? How was he important to the morale, the spirit, and the imagination of postwar America?

15. The press seemed to adore Stubby in the postwar years, and reporters played a significant role in making his story legendary in scope. Why would this narrative be important to the media? Why would they be eager to embellish the facts?

16. How did Stubby's physical characteristics and overall nature help him survive on the battlefields of the First World War? How did they help him in his postwar years?

17. Stubby's fame coincided with the public's increasing love of dogs (page 157). Why did dogs gain in popularity as pets at that time? Which of Stubby's qualities would have been attractive and inspirational to ordinary citizens in search of animal companionship?

18. The honors Stubby received after the war drew sporadic criticism during an era when many veterans faced difficulties transitioning to civilian life (pages 169). How would veterans who knew Stubby have responded to this criticism? Why did Stubby continue to be an important symbol of their service even after the war had ended?

19. Robert Conroy may have missed his calling as a publicist. He established exceptional political connections and had a knack for managing the news media. What tactics did he employ to keep Stubby in the public eye throughout their postwar lives? Did he use any strategies that might be considered inappropriate by today's standards?

20. A *New Britain Herald* writer said, "Stubby was the concentration of all we like in human beings and lacked everything we dislike in

them" (page 187). Which of Stubby's qualities would have made him, as the *Herald* writer goes on to say, "the visible incarnation of the great spirit that hovered over the 26th"? If Stubby represented the best in human beings, what were some of the traits he lacked that can be seen as unlikable in humans (or animals)?

21. According to the National Institute of Mental Health, one of the warning signs of post-traumatic stress disorder (PTSD) is when an individual exhibits symptoms that make it difficult to negotiate the challenges of daily life, including going to school or work, being with friends and family, and taking care of important tasks. Does Robert Conroy seem to have experienced PTSD?

22. The National Center for PTSD warns against certain coping behaviors that may do more harm than good for those with symptoms of the disorder. The list of *negative coping* behaviors includes such things as avoiding others, avoiding memories of the traumatic event, and working too much. How could a pet like Stubby help veterans avoid negative coping?

23. What would the reasons be for adding a memorial to military service dogs to the Vietnam Veterans Memorial in Washington, D.C.? What would the arguments be against the addition? Who would benefit from such a memorial and why?

24. Although World War I serves as a backdrop for most of the book, the text conveys a love story along with the war story. In what ways is this book about love? Does this theme extend beyond the relationship between Stubby and Robert Conroy?

25. What is it about the history of Robert Conroy and Stubby that continues to resonate today? Why are we inspired by stories about the bonds between humans and animals? What qualities do dogs offer, uniquely from other animals, to their human companions?

DISCOVER MORE HEROES
from National Geographic

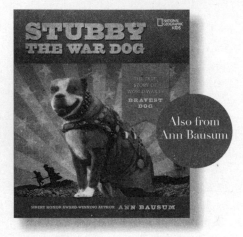

Also from
Ann Bausum

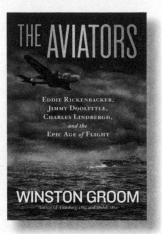

 Packed with period photographs, family memorabilia, and vintage artwork, Ann Bausum's *Stubby the War Dog* tells the true story of WWI's bravest dog, for ages 10 and up.

The saga of three extraordinary aviators—Charles Lindbergh, Eddie Rickenbacker, and Jimmy Doolittle—and how they redefined heroism through their genius, daring, and uncommon courage.

History will be made in this lifetime—by following a road map to Mars from a man who has traveled to the moon and back.

AVAILABLE WHEREVER BOOKS ARE SOLD
nationalgeographic.com/books